365 Steps to Self-Confidence

365

steps to
self-confidence

David Lawrence Preston

howtobooks

Published by How To Books Ltd,
3 Newtec Place, Magdalen Road,
Oxford OX4 1RE. United Kingdom.
Tel: (01865) 793806. Fax: (01865) 248780
email: info@howtobooks.co.uk
http://www.howtobooks.co.uk

First edition 2001
Second edition 2005

British Library Cataloguing in Publication Data.
A catalogue record for this book is available from the British Library.

Produced for How To Books by Deer Park Productions, Tavistock
Typeset and design by Pantek Arts Ltd, Maidstone
Printed and bound in Great Britain, by Bell & Bain Ltd, Glasgow

NOTE: The material contained in this book is set out in good faith for general guidance and no liability can be accepted for loss or expense incurred as a result of relying in particular circumstances on statements made in this book. Laws and regulations are complex and liable to change, and readers should check the current position with the relevant authorities before making personal arrangements.

Dedication

This book is dedicated to my wonderful children, Dieter, Nikki, Dan and Joel, to whom I wish all the health, happiness and success in the world.

Acknowledgements

With grateful thanks to my dear friends Janet Chiesa, for her numerous valuable suggestions and comments, and Christine Simpson, Pam Hanley and Marc Batistella for coming to my rescue when I had problems with my computer just before the publisher's deadline!

Introduction

'A man who doubts himself is like a man who enlists in the ranks of the enemy and bears arms against himself. He makes his failure certain by being the first to be convinced of it.'
Alexandre Dumas

CONFIDENCE IS CRUCIAL TO A HAPPY AND FULFILLING LIFE. It influences your success at work, your family life, relationships and leisure activities. It affects your performance in everything you do. A belief in one's self is without doubt the greatest asset of all. Even great wealth and fame can't compensate for a poor self-image.

People who lack confidence and self-belief *always* underachieve. They're less adventurous and less likely to get the most out of life. They're more prone to a variety of stress-related problems, including anxiety, eating disorders and mental health problems. Low self-esteem is the fundamental cause of most family break-ups, poor parenting and relationship problems. In addition, much crime is associated with drug abuse, unemployment, poverty and aimlessness, all of which are related to low self-esteem.

Does lack of confidence hold you back? If so, you've made a wise purchase. *365 Steps to Self Confidence* has been carefully structured to help you become more confident. It takes you deep inside your mind and gives you tools and techniques which have worked for millions of people around the world. All you have to do is to work through and apply its lessons.

Time and energy devoted to building your confidence and self-esteem are nothing less than investments in your whole life. The exciting thing is, no matter what your history, background or current state of confidence, you – we all – can learn to be confident, because *it's never too late.*

A Personal Note

Most of the people I meet in my work perceive themselves as not capable of much. Some don't even particularly like themselves. I know how they feel. As a young man I felt the same, and it nearly destroyed me before I acquired the confidence to become a teacher, therapist and organiser of personal development and complementary therapy courses.

I've always thought that if low self-esteem were *a physical* condition such as cancer or AIDS, or a potentially life-threatening habit like smoking and alcohol and drug abuse, the government would declare a national emergency, pump in massive funds and organise a mass publicity campaign to combat it. Certainly some politicians and educationalists are beginning to pay lip service to it, and hopefully times are changing.

But in all my years of full-time education, at school, college and university, *I can't recall a single session on self-esteem.* Nor in a 20-year business career were any training resources devoted to it. No one seemed to recognise its importance. Perhaps everyone assumed that nothing could be done, or vaguely hoped that confidence would develop as a by-product of other activities.

I would like to see courses in confidence and self-esteem made compulsory in all schools and colleges. All teachers, student teachers and anyone who regularly comes into contact with young people should be fully trained in the subject, including parents and would-be parents.

If this were given priority, who knows what could be achieved? How many lives would be enriched? Our nation could be transformed from the grass roots up within a generation. Now wouldn't that be exciting?

About this book

I have written this book for everyone – young and old, men, women, students, educators, business people, administrators, parents, homemakers, sports enthusiasts, entertainers – yes, and you!

It has been carefully structured into 52 sections, covering the following areas:

- Deciding to be confident
- Self-awareness
- Thinking confidently
- Using your imagination to improve self-image
- Acting with confidence
- Confident communication.

Each section contains information, insights and words of inspiration, plus seven exercises, practical hints or points to ponder. That's one a day – not too taxing. is it?

I guarantee that if you read the material carefully and apply what you learn, you'll notice big changes taking place within two or three months, and a year from now you'll look back amazed at how much more confident you've become.

The Programme

Section

1 How to build confidence – an overview

The formula for building confidence, indeed for bringing about any personal change, has five elements.

First, develop **self-awareness**: know yourself, acknowledge that there are aspects of yourself that you wish to change, and understand what has stopped you feeling confident so far.

Then apply the **ITIA Formula**© (pronounced eye-tea-ah):

- Assert your **intention** to be confident, and make a commitment.
- Change your **thinking**. This includes changing restrictive attitudes and beliefs.
- Use your **imagination**. Imagine yourself as a confident person.
- **Act** as if you are already confident. The more you speak and behave confidently, the more confident you will become.

All four parts of the ITIA Formula© are essential, otherwise the change is unlikely to be permanent, or worse, nothing may change at all.

If this sounds a little daunting, don't worry – this entire programme is designed around these five elements – self-awareness, intention, thinking, imagination and acting 'as if'. You will be introduced to them in small, practical steps to make it as easy as possible for you. All I ask is that you apply what you learn, stick with it and be patient. Entrenched habits don't change overnight.

Self-esteem isn't everything, it's just that there's nothing without it

Gloria Steinem

1 Our first step is a simple but necessary one: buy a medium sized notebook. Use it for the written exercises in this programme, also to record your experiences and monitor your progress. Date each entry you make.

Your notebook will become a good friend, teacher and confidant, so keep it near you, consult it every day and update it regularly.

Commit yourself to spending some time on this programme every day. Just ten minutes a day – reading, learning, thinking, doing etc – adds up to over 60 valuable hours of confidence building activity a year from now. Twenty-five minutes a day builds up to 152 hours in a year – that's almost a week! Can you think of a better investment for your future?

2 What difference would it make to your life if you *knew* without any doubt that you could achieve anything you set your heart on? If you like jot down a few comments in your notebook.

3 Think about, and if you like write down, what confidence means to you. What do confident people do that unconfident people do not? What would you do differently if you were confident?

For example, perhaps you would find it easier to speak up for yourself, show your emotions, meet new people, or take on more responsibility at work?

4 Write down three beliefs that you hold about yourself which could be limiting your confidence.

Now think of three beliefs you would rather have, beliefs that would empower you and bring confidence. Cross out the limiting beliefs and write these empowering beliefs in their place.

What would you have to do for these new beliefs to come true?

5 Make yourself very comfortable, either sitting or lying down. Close your eyes, take a few deep breaths and relax.

Allow your imagination to flow freely. What would it be like to be perfectly confident? What difference would it make to your life?

Let your mind drift for a few minutes, then open your eyes and write down everything that comes to mind. Keep this list: you have it in your power to experience all this one day. Remember, whatever your mind can conceive and believe, you *can* achieve.

6 Commit yourself to behaving more confidently, as from *now*, even if it feels like an act. Do what actors, musicians, politicians, sports stars and many others do the world over – *pretend* you're confident, even if you're not.

For instance, calm your breath, stand upright, look people in the eye and speak with a clear, unwavering tone: you will immediately feel more confident.

7 From now on make this an unshakable rule: *stop putting yourself down.* Never say anything about yourself, either silently or out loud, that you don't sincerely want to *be* or *come true.*

Decide right now to treat yourself with love and respect and accept only the best for yourself for the rest of your life.

Behind their public personae many well known people, including the most glamorous and esteemed, are desperately shy.

In a recent radio broadcast Terry O'Neill, the celebrity photographer whose pictures of the rich and famous have adorned glossy magazines all over the world, described the Paramount Studios' centenary celebrations in Hollywood. A hundred top movie stars were brought together, many of whom wanted to meet Elizabeth Taylor. O'Neill spotted her cowering in a corner, close to the door.

'I thought, no one's going near her,' he said, 'so, as I'd met her before, I asked if I could assist her. I pointed out that all those people were here to meet her. She said, "I'm so frightened, Terry. I've never seen so many stars in one room." She was star struck – they all were! Then she asked me to introduce her to Robert de Niro. I didn't know him, but I took her over, and it was amazing. It was like seeing two stumbling children talking with each other.'

2 How confident are you?

How confident are you? What is confidence anyway, and how does it relate to self-esteem and self-image?

Your self-image – the way you see yourself – is made up of three core feelings and beliefs:

- **Self-worth**: the value you place on yourself – how comfortable you are being you and the extent to which you feel worthy of happiness and success.

- **Competence**: your beliefs about your capacity to achieve, solve problems and think for yourself. This is what I mean by *confidence*.

- **Belonging**: whether you feel accepted and respected by others.

Your assessment of your self-worth and feelings of belonging make up your *self-esteem*.

Your aim is, of course, to make confidence such a natural part of yourself that you not only appear confident on the *outside* but also feel completely at ease with yourself *inside*. This is only achieved when all four elements of the ITIA Formula© are combined. Intention and thought have a direct impact on *confidence*, which is basically a set of *beliefs* about your talents and capabilities. But they have little effect on *self-worth*, which is primarily emotional in nature, and as we all know, intention and thought have little influence over the emotions.

This is where imagination and action come in. Your creative imagination has a direct effect on the emotions and, providing they are pursued in the right spirit, so do your actions.

Now, to return to my original question, how's your self-worth? Do you believe you're competent to cope with life and achieve? And do you feel accepted and respected by others?

If you deliberately plan to be less than you are capable of being, then I warn you that you will be unhappy for the rest of your life. You'll be evading your own capabilities, your own possibilities.

Professor Abraham Maslow

8

How confident are you? Give yourself a mark out of ten, where ten means you feel you can achieve anything you desire (if you apply yourself), and zero, that you feel totally incapable of anything. (If you award yourself ten, give this book to a friend – you obviously don't need it!)

Now give yourself a mark for how high you would like your confidence to be. If you give yourself less than ten, ask yourself why. Reflect on the mark you have given yourself.

9

How high is your self-worth? Give yourself a mark out of ten, where ten means you feel worthy of all the good things life has to offer, and zero, you feel completely worthless and undeserving. Now give yourself a mark for how high you would like it to be. Again, if you give yourself less than ten ask yourself why and reflect on the mark you have given yourself.

10

Do you feel that you are well respected by others? Give yourself a mark out of ten for how well you relate to others. Now give yourself a mark for how well you would like to relate to others. Once again, if you give yourself less than ten ask yourself why and reflect on the mark you have given yourself.

11 Take a large piece of paper and draw a line down the middle. At the top on the left write down your first name, or the name by which you are best known (which could be a nickname). Underneath, describe how you feel about this name.

Now choose a name by which you would like to be known. Write it at the top of the right-hand column. Who is this person? Fill this side of the page with notes about him or her, who you imagine them to be. Then compare the two columns. What does this tell you?

12 Award yourself marks out of ten for how satisfied you are with:

- Your *physical* attributes: health, fitness and appearance.

- Your *emotional* make-up: are you happy, a loving person, caring and considerate, calm and secure?

- Your *intellect*: your intelligence, skills and qualifications.

- Your *social skills*: how comfortable you feel in social situations and what you believe others think of you.

Reflect on why you have given yourself these marks.

13 Write down what your potential is. What could you achieve if you had loads of confidence?

One thing is certain – you are capable of far more than you think. Most people's idea of their capabilities bears little relation to their actual potential.

14 Smile at yourself in the mirror every morning; you'll be surprised what a difference it can make to your day.

And smile at yourself at night before retiring, as this brings sweet dreams and programmes your subconscious mind to feel good about yourself.

'One moment I was living in a leaky shoe box...'

Not long ago I was invited to take part in a radio phone-in. As I was ushered into the studio the presenter looked up from the console, ran his eyes over me, then stood up and shook my hand. 'Welcome', he smiled. 'I must say, you don't look like the sort of slink-pot who writes books on confidence.'

I knew exactly what he meant. We've all seen those silky-smooth characters with designer suits, perfect hair and cosmetic teeth beaming at us from the glossy covers of self-help books and magazines.

I have great respect for the work of some of these people, but many of them come across, by their actions if not by their words, as having one main interest in life – making money, and lots of it. Some are like the character in the Monty Python sketch: 'One moment I was living in a shoe box in the gutter, then I discovered *the secret*, and 12 months later I owned a chateau overlooking the sea, a fleet of stretch limousines and a private plane, a holiday home on a tropical island and an ocean-going yacht. I'd met and married the perfect woman and we're well on the way to having six perfect children.'

Whether or not you wish to emulate such people is, of course, a personal matter, as long as you don't delude yourself into thinking you will automatically find happiness and peace of mind merely by accumulating wealth. This is not what confidence is about. Confident people have no need to show off, or impose themselves on others. They may have high expectations of themselves, but they also know their self-worth is independent of their achievements and that they don't always have to be perfect....

and they don't have to be slink pots!

3 Sow the seeds of confidence and watch them grow

What you sow you reap is a time-honoured truism. If you plant an acorn in moist, fertile soil, it will grow into a mighty oak. It can't help it, it's genetically programmed that way.

Similarly, no matter what has gone before, if you plant the seeds of confidence in your consciousness through your intentions, thoughts, attitudes and beliefs, imaginings, actions and words, and keep them well nourished, confidence will grow.

You'll notice I said *no matter what has gone before.* Certainly you have been influenced by past events and circumstances, but they do not tell the whole story. The seeds – or causes – that have blossomed into the person you are include:

■ Your genetic inheritance and biochemistry (hormones etc). Scientists tell us that these account for around 25-35% of your character.

■ The environment in which you were raised, including people.

■ Your unique way of trying to make sense of it all, both at the time and now.

Obviously you cannot change your genes, and you cannot change your biochemistry without resorting to drastic, potentially dangerous measures (drugs etc). But if greater confidence is your aim, there's no need. Because although your genetic inheritance is known to play a role in determining how outgoing you are, whether you are volatile or placid, and your predisposition for certain mental health problems (such as stress, depression, addictions and compulsive behaviours), **no causal link has ever been found between genes and confidence**.

Confidence (or lack of it) is *learned*, mostly in the first few years of childhood. It began to take shape when you were weak and vulnerable, after which it became self-reinforcing. And anything which has been learned can be reappraised and replaced with new, superior learning.

Yesterday is but a dream
And tomorrow only a vision
But today well lived makes
Every yesterday a dream of happiness
And every tomorrow a vision of hope
Look well therefore to this day.

Traditional Indian Poem

15 Promise yourself that from now on you'll sow only 'seeds' – positive thoughts, fantasies and mental images, words and actions – that boost your confidence, improve your relationships and make you feel good about yourself.

16 List some of the factors in your life – including past events, people and situations – which have affected your confidence. In what way did they affect you?

Now, without making any judgements, consider how your attitudes and beliefs, fantasies, communication style and actions have created your life. Write down anything that seems relevant.

17 Do you consider yourself predominantly an introvert or an extrovert? In other words, do you enjoy your own company and easily get drawn into your own inner world? Or do you get most of your energy and inspiration from the company of others?

You can be confident either way, and you certainly don't have to be loud and gregarious. Being quietly confident is just as rewarding.

18   Commit yourself to *doing* whatever it takes to become more confident.
I know many who enjoy discussing the reasons for their lack of
confidence, but do nothing about it. *Don't be one of them.*

Write these words on a sticky label or small card and place it where
you will see it first thing each day:

'I greet every new day with a firm commitment to raising my
confidence. I will do whatever is required to become more confident.'

Whenever you see these words, smile and repeat them to yourself,
with conviction, silently or aloud, at least ten times. Say them as if you
really mean it.

19   Think of one thing you would like to do that makes you nervous –
nothing too demanding at this stage. Tell yourself over and over again,
'I am enjoying (doing whatever it is). I know I *can* do it, and I will.'

20   Make yourself very comfortable, either sitting or lying down. Close
your eyes, take a few deep breaths and allow your imagination to flow
freely. Imagine that you have loads of confidence and are actually doing
whatever it is that makes you nervous.

After a few minutes, open your eyes. Write down anything that
comes to mind in your notebook.

21   Now, if practical, go ahead and do what you imagined in Confidence
Builder 20. Don't be put off by any uncomfortable feelings that arise.

You've just put the ITIA Formula© into practice for the very first
time. How do you feel?

'What would my mother say?'

At 52 years of age George Stratford was sleeping rough on a park bench, jobless, penniless and feeling too old to make a new life. Then one morning he woke with a start, haunted by the thought, 'What would my mother say if she could see this bum I've turned into?'

It made him *think*. He stopped feeling sorry for himself and became determined to sort himself out. He thought of the novel he had started several years earlier and never completed, and affirmed his *intention* to finish it and get it published.

His *imagination* wandered to his dream of becoming a novelist. How wonderful it would be to be a famous author!

Then he took *action*. He enrolled at a local college to study English, and the following year won a place on an advertising course after submitting the first two chapters of his novel. Then he spent the last of his savings on the train fare to London to take up a work experience placement at a top advertising agency, and despite sleeping rough at this time, was taken on by them on a permanent basis. Simultaneously he wrote a minimum of 1,000 words a day until his novel was finished.

The culmination of George's efforts was the launch of his novel, In *The Long Run*, at a star-studded reception in London. Set against the backdrop of the Comrades' Marathon in South Africa, one of the world's most arduous races, it explores the themes of confidence, courage and determination – qualities which the author demonstrates in abundance!

4 Whose responsibility?

Only one person can build your confidence – guess who? That's right, *you*. If you don't do it, who will?

It will only happen if you make a firm commitment, set goals, plan a strategy and take action. All of this means *accepting full responsibility* for yourself – deciding to be confident and refusing to allow anyone to deflect you from your chosen course.

Accepting responsibility adds up to never, never blaming other people for:

- Your lack of confidence
- How others treat you
- Your thoughts, words and actions
- Failures, misfortunes and setbacks
- *Or anything else.*

Assume that everything that happens from now on is your own doing. Think and behave accordingly. You'll find it's one of the most liberating things you can do.

For any of us to be truly free, we must first be willing to be responsible for our lives.

David McNally

---

22 Consider why people find it so hard to admit full responsibility for their lives? What are they afraid of?

Does any of this apply to you? Think of a time when you didn't take responsibility. Write down what you were afraid of.

---

23 Write down this sentence:

'I avoid self-responsibility the most when...'

Quickly, without thinking about it too hard, write down the first six things that come to mind. Reflect on what you've written. What does it tell you about yourself?

---

24 Write down this sentence:

'If I took more responsibility for my thoughts, words and actions...'

Quickly write down the first six things that come to mind. Reflect on what you've written. What have you learned?

25 Create a **Wall of Confidence**. To change erroneous beliefs it's necessary to keep reminding yourself of what is right and true, so why not cover one wall of your home with your favourite confidence-boosting ideas, quotations and anecdotes? If you prefer, put up a noticeboard.

Whenever you come across an inspiring or a constructive idea, pin it up. You don't have to learn them off by heart – simply having them on display influences the subconscious.

Start by posting these affirmations on your Wall of Confidence.

'It is *safe* for me to take charge of my life.'

'*I am responsible* for myself and everything I think and do.'

26 Think of three things you can do or stop doing from now on to take responsibility for your confidence and self-esteem. Write them out in large script, in the form of a poster, and fix it to your Wall of Confidence.

27 Resolve to face up to problems and difficulties rather than avoiding them. Avoiding pain and discomfort – physical and emotional – is understandable, but self-defeating in the longer term. You merely find yourself being confronted by similar difficulties over and over again until you eventually have to face up to them. *And it does nothing for your confidence.*

28 From now on accept full responsibility for your feelings – *all* of them. Look at yourself in a mirror and say, 'Today, and for the rest of my life, I am responsible for my own feelings. I am in charge of my emotions.' *Do it now!*

We have to learn to be our own best friend because we fall too easily into the trap of being our own worst enemies.

Roderick Thorp

You have the power....

You have the power to become confident, if you want to, and if you go about it the right way. Everyone has this power and it doesn't matter how lacking in confidence you are now.

You can change your way of thinking. You can use your imagination differently. You can alter your way of speaking. You can let go of destructive habits and change your behaviour. You can do all this now, from this moment on. Then over time your confidence will grow and you'll feel better and better about yourself with each passing day.

How do I know?

Firstly because I know hundreds of people *personally* who have become more confident, and I know of thousands more.

Secondly, they include the person with whom I spend the most time – myself. In my teens I had no confidence whatsoever. I couldn't even bring myself to say hello to people I didn't know. Then, in my mid-20s, I decided to do something about it. I started reading self-help books and attending courses and seminars. I worked on myself. I've since accomplished many things I could not have envisaged in those far off days, including speaking to large audiences. I have far exceeded my initial expectations. And I'm still improving.

I'm no different from you. If I can do it, so can you!

Every single step makes a difference, so start right away. Take responsibility. Sow the seeds of confidence and watch them grow. Millions have already done so and now it's your turn!

5 Getting Motivated

Building confidence takes time, patience and effort. You will have to take a few risks. At times you will feel anxious. How can you motivate yourself to put up with the discomfort and persevere?

We humans are motivated by:

- **A want or need** which induces tension. Only if these are *un*satisfied can there be motivational power.

- **Perceptions of 'pleasure' and 'pain'.** We seek pleasure and are driven by a desire to avoid pain.

- **Hopes and expectations** that we can get what we want, and that everything *will* come right in the end.

The strongest motivation comes from a passionate desire for something pleasurable, coupled with the avoidance of pain.

The best way to motivate yourself is to set yourself some worthy goals, find plenty of reasons why you want to accomplish them, and keep in mind the consequences of failure – which is what you are about to do.

Goals are so important that I shall assume for the rest of this programme that you have several on the go at all times. More about them in Section 29.

To change one's life: Start immediately. Do it flamboyantly.
No exceptions. No excuses.

Professor William James

29 Ask yourself, 'What am I trying to achieve by believing I lack confidence?' Write down the answers.

A difficult one, this. You may have to be more honest with yourself than you're used to; but don't skip over it just because it makes you feel uncomfortable – your answers may illuminate and surprise you.

30 Write down this sentence:

'If I had an excellent self-image and total confidence in my abilities, I would...'

Write down whatever comes to mind.

31 Take each item on your list from Confidence Builder 30 and make it a firm goal. Write it in the form:

'My goal is to...'

Commit yourself unreservedly to working towards these goals.

32 Make yourself very comfortable, either sitting or lying down. Close your eyes, take a few deep breaths and allow your imagination to flow freely. Imagine you have accomplished the goals you set yourself in confidence Builder 31. Visualise them coming true in every detail. How do you feel?

When you open your eyes write down any thoughts that come into your head.

33 Think of something you can do as a first step towards each goal set in Confidence Builder 31, one action you can take to get the ball rolling – even if it's just making a short phone call or reading a relevant magazine article – *and do it now*. No exceptions, no excuses!

34 Write the following affirmation on a small card and carry it with you. Repeat it silently or out loud, at least ten times, three or four times a day:
'I think, speak and act confidently at all times.'
More about affirmations in Section 10.

35 Take a trip to your local library or book shop, find the self-help shelves and browse. There are dozens of excellent self-help books, chock full of information and ideas. Make your choice, and spend a few moments every day reading useful, inspiring material or listening to tape programmes. (There is a recommended reading/listening list on page 223.)

'It feels really good to do something for myself'

One person who was motivated to change was Lynne. She had lived by other people's rules for most of her life, usually allowing others to make decisions on her behalf. Then one evening, after a heated row, her abusive and manipulative husband of 20 years stormed out in a rage, threatening to throw himself over a cliff. He expected her to beg him to return, as she had always done before. But unbeknown to him she had been quietly working on her confidence and this time she refused. At first he threatened, then he pleaded, but she held firm.

This was the beginning of a new phase in her life. Six months later, no longer facing the daily outbursts which she had previously endured, her home was a haven of calm. She had taken computing lessons, found a well paid job, enrolled for evening art classes, and was performing with a local group of singers. Even her son, no longer having to endure the tension, was happier and more settled at school.

'Since I worked on my confidence,' Lynne said, 'I feel as if I'm in control. It feels really good to do something for myself that I've always wanted to do. And I know if I don't I've only got myself to blame'.

6 Determination

Determination is perhaps the quality that underpins *all* success. No one gets very far without it. If you've lacked confidence for years it won't change overnight without determination on your part.

Every choice you make – including the choice to become more confident – is a result of weighing up the balance of 'pleasure' and 'pain'. When faced with a decision, you consciously or subconsciously weigh up the alternatives and their consequences. You ask yourself:

- What are the advantages of pursuing this course of action? If I go ahead, what will be the probable rewards? How much 'pleasure' will it bring? Are there any disadvantages? How much 'pain'?

- If I do *not go* ahead, how much 'pain' will I avoid? And how much 'pleasure' am I likely to forego?

For example, learning a new skill potentially brings many future benefits, but may involve short-term sacrifices, especially the time and effort you put in. *But as long as you keep in mind the advantages that will come your way, your determination remains strong.* Anything is possible if you have enough reasons to change.

It only takes 30 days to lay the foundations for lasting change in your thinking, your behaviour and your life.

'If you head towards your goal with courage and determination, all the powers of the universe will come to your aid.'

Ralph Waldo Emerson

36 Write a few notes on the advantages of staying as you are and *not* becoming more confident, both for yourself and others. For example, your friends and family may prefer you passive and compliant. What reasons are there for remaining in your present comfort zone?

You'll find this exercise remarkably thought-provoking.

37 List at least ten benefits to *you personally* of your becoming more confident. How much 'pleasure' will it bring? Think about your work, your career, your social relationships and family life, leisure pursuits, health, and your mental, emotional and spiritual wellbeing.

Then add the benefits of your increase in confidence to other people. For example, your family could benefit in numerous ways from being associated with a new, more confident you.

38 List at least ten reasons why staying as you are is unacceptable. What will you miss out on? How much 'pleasure' will you forego?

39 Now consider the price to be paid – the time, effort, stress and uncertainty – that accompanies change. Consider these questions:

■ What must I do to build my confidence?

■ What price must I expect to pay for becoming more confident?

■ How much effort will it take? How much effort am I willing to make?

40 In Confidence Builders 36-39 you have identified:

- The rewards of becoming confident.
- The advantages of staying as you are.
- The *dis*advantages of *not* changing.
- The *dis*advantages of becoming more confident.

Reflect on these. What have you learned?

41 Summarise the benefits of becoming more confident on a small card. Carry it with you and read them aloud every day for the next 30 days. Make them into a small poster and display it on your Wall of Confidence. The card and poster will reinforce your determination, especially when your quest for confidence takes you into uncharted waters.

42 Make this your motto:

'From now on I *intend* to be confident. My confidence *must* change; *I* must change it; and l *can*.'

Say it out loud. As you recite it, smile knowingly to yourself. It will soon be firmly imprinted on your memory.

'Feel the fear and do it anyway'

There's no better example of determination and persistence than author Dr Susan Jeffers.

Married at 18, by the age of 25 she felt trapped in a life of tedious domesticity. Believing she was meant to be doing something in addition to raising a family, she enrolled at university, gaining a B.A. and an M.A. six years later. By the mid-seventies she had become the Director of New York's Floating Hospital, an educational and medical facility for the disadvantaged. It was there she began her journey into self-discovery that eventually led to her writing her first million selling self-help book, *Feel The Fear And Do It Anyway*.

Written in 1986, *Feel The Fear...* was mocked and rejected by most of the major publishers, who had no experience of this type of book. One told her, 'Lady Di could be cycling nude down the street giving this book away and still nobody would read it.'

But she was determined to succeed. 'If an idea is a pioneering one,' she observed, 'it often seems foolish and flies in the face of established wisdom.' Now, thanks in no small part to her efforts, the self-help genre is a well-established and much appreciated section of the book trade.

7 Think like a confident person

Now it's time to take a close look at how you think.

As the greatest and wisest teachers have always taught, improving the quality of your thoughts improves your life almost immediately:

- The Bible quotes King Solomon: 'As a man thinketh, so shall he be.'

- The Buddhist text, The Dhammapada, states: 'We are what we think. All that we are arises with our thoughts. With our thoughts, we make our world.'

- The Greek philosopher Socrates said, 'To find yourself, think for yourself.'

When you think like a confident person, you automatically feel more confident and act more confidently. Positive thinkers are the happiest and most successful. *Sometimes all it takes to change your life forever is a single thought!*

Humans are not robots: you can intentionally choose how to think, and if you are serious about building your confidence you must start changing your thinking patterns without delay. The next few sections explain how.

Unless there be correct thought, there cannot be any action, and when there is correct thought, right action will follow.'

Henry George

43 When you think like a confident person you *feel* more confident and *act* more confidently, so *commit yourself* to taking charge of your thoughts. Write this sentence on a small card and repeat it to yourself, with conviction, several times a day:

'I am a positive thinker – I think and talk confidently at all times.'

44 Consider: Are you a negative thinker? A killjoy? Do you find it difficult to think positively? Does your conversation often take on an air of doom and gloom? This awareness is critical to your wellbeing now and in the future, so be totally honest with yourself.

45 If the answers to the questions in Confidence Builder 44 is no, give yourself a pat on the back and promise to continue as a positive thinker.

If the answers are yes, reflect:

- What has my negative thinking brought me so far?

- How different would I be if I were more positive in my outlook?

Write down at least six differences that being more positive would make to your life.

46

You become aware of your conscious thoughts as a running commentary playing inside your head – your self-talk or internal dialogue. Taking charge of your thinking is, in fact, simply changing what you say to yourself.

Aim to manage your 'internal dialogue' so that you talk to yourself in a positive and uplifting fashion all the time. This may take a little practice, but it's easily possible. *Becoming an habitually confident thinker is no more difficult than learning to ride a bicycle.*

47

Practise making sentences which start with assertive statements such as 'I can', 'I am', 'I want', '1 do', and 'I choose'.

48

Promise yourself that from now on you will never:

■ Put yourself down.

■ Say you can't.

■ Say that what you want is impossible.

■ Tell yourself that you are incapable of learning anything new.

49

'Yes!' is one of the most powerful affirmations you can make. Say it often, with enthusiasm. Display it in big letters on your Wall of Confidence. Say it whenever a new opportunity comes your way. And – try this and notice the difference it makes – say it with relish when you face a difficult problem or challenge.

Thought can become a powerful instrument of self-liberation in the hands of one taught to use it properly.'

Dr Paul Brunton

Image consultant Marcia Grad spells out the importance of changing your thinking patterns with crystal clarity in her book, *Charisma: How to Get that Special Magic*.

'As long as you keep thinking as you've been thinking, you'll keep feeling as you've been feeling, doing as you've been doing, and getting what you've been getting.'

8 The Four Step Method

Negative thinking can quickly spiral out of control and destroy your confidence if you allow it. This is where **The Four Step Method** – a simple technique for becoming aware of disempowering thoughts – comes in. It's quickly learned and easily applied and, with practice, soon becomes second nature.

The four steps are:

1. Be mindful.

2. Stop disempowering thoughts.

3. Replace them with empowering thoughts.

4. Keep going until it becomes automatic.

The Four Step Method is quite simply *the most effective single technique I know for building self-confidence.* If this programme teaches you nothing else, you will still change your life permanently for the better.

Choose your own thoughts. Don't let anyone else choose them for you.

David Lawrence Preston

50 | Memorise the Four Step Method. Recite it out loud until you know it off by heart.

51 | Practise mindfulness. Mindfulness means paying attention to what you are thinking and feeling, and being aware of how you respond to people and events.

When you become more mindful your mind becomes quieter and you see things more clearly. You are less likely to speak and act hastily. Mindfulness deepens your understanding of yourself and the world around you. It is a vital step towards greater confidence and self-esteem.

52 | For the next five minutes (time yourself), do just one thing at once and verbalise every movement you make. For example:

'Now I am thinking about picking up my pen.
Now I am picking up my pen.
Now I am writing in my notebook.
Now I put the pen down.
Now I close the book.
Now I put the book in the drawer.'

Do this daily for the next seven days. It will seem strange at first – but do it anyway. It's a powerful exercise in mindfulness.

53 For the next seven days stop what you're doing for five minutes a day, be quiet and still, and listen in on your thoughts. Don't try to interrupt: just let the thoughts come and go of their own accord, as if they're happening to someone else.

You probably won't find this easy at first. The untrained, unsettled mind has a tendency to flit from one thing to another, and even 60 seconds' conscious attention seems like an eternity when you're not used to it.

54 If you have a watch that bleeps on the hour, take this as a signal to stop what you're doing and practise mindfulness just for one minute. If safe to do so, close your eyes and listen to the incessant chattering of the mind. Then resume your activities.

55 Notice whether anyone with whom you come into contact, or specific events, either affect you physically, trigger uncomfortable feelings, or spark off a train of self-doubting thoughts. Make a written note of anything significant.

56 Write down all the reasons why you would find it difficult to start applying the Four Step Method right away. The Four Step Method is so easy!

Be a good mother to your mind

'Learning to talk properly to the self is a
Spiritual endeavour. Thoughts from the past and
worries about the future do not create good
conversation. Instead, learn to talk to your
mind as if it were a child. Talk to it with love.

If you force a child to sit down, he won't.
A good mother knows how to prompt her child
into doing what she wants. Be a good mother
to your mind; teach it good, positive thoughts
so that when you tell it to sit quietly, it will.'

Dadi Janki

9 Silencing the Inner Critic

The Inner Critic is that pernicious little voice inside your head that constantly carps, complains and condemns. It is the voice that sows doubt – 'Yes... but.... supposing. You're rubbish at that, you know you are. It will all go wrong, it always does!'

If you let thoughts such as these go unchallenged you give the Inner Critic the power to destroy your confidence and lower your self-esteem. You must learn to tell it to shut up, stop being silly and go away. Then change the thoughts to something positive.

This is the second of the Four Steps, *Thought Stopping*. It can be used in any instant, and has an immediate effect. This way you may not prevent negative thoughts entering your mind, but you can render them powerless.

Don't be afraid of your negative thoughts: just know them for what they are – not the truth, just negative thoughts. Give them no house room in your consciousness and they will dissolve into what they are – false ideas, false concepts, with nothing to sustain them.

Nona Coxhead

57 As you listen in on your self-talk, step back and observe. Ask yourself. 'Why am I thinking that thought? Where is it taking me? Does it help me feel confident?'

58 When you become aware of a negative thought, use Thought Stopping. Interrupt the unwanted thought by saying firmly. 'No!' 'Stop!' 'Go away!' 'Delete!' or some other word or phrase of your choice. Do this silently or aloud (out loud is best, if circumstances permit).

59 The mind is not a vacuum; you cannot *not* think. Moreover, you can only think one conscious thought at a time (if you don't believe me, try thinking two thoughts at once – impossible!). So once you've dispensed with the *unwanted* thought immediately replace it with another, to prevent another unwanted thought popping into your conscious mind.

If you can't think of an appropriate thought immediately, use an affirmation, such as:

'I like myself.'
'I am a strong and worthy person.'
'I'm perfect just as I am.'

60 Now take the Thought Stopping technique a stage further. As you detach yourself from an unwanted thought, simultaneously stamp your feet, pinch yourself, slap your thigh or bang on a table etc. Be sensible: obviously there are times and places when this is inconvenient, or even dangerous, so use your discretion.

61 Try this alternative form of Thought Stopping. When you notice a disempowering thought, have a good snigger to yourself: just laugh at its nonsense. Say, 'So you're the thought? Ha! Ha!', or 'Oops! There goes another one!' Then allow yourself a warm inner smile.

62 Make yourself very comfortable, either sitting or lying down. Close your eyes. take a few deep breaths and imagine there is a little person sweeping up the doubting, anxious, useless, self-deprecating thoughts into a pile of dust in the centre of your head. When they're all swept up, 'blow' the dust out of your mouth and 'watch' it disperse into the atmosphere.

Affirm to yourself that the negative thoughts won't trouble you again. Notice how you feel. This works particularly well when you are stressed or anxious.

63 When you first use the Four Step Formula you will encounter resistance. Your subconscious wants to hang on to existing habits, because this is how it's designed to operate. If it tries to sabotage your progress for instance, by making you feel as if you're lying to yourself, *don't let it!*

It takes about a month to change a thinking pattern permanently, so keep at it, be patient and don't castigate yourself if you slip up. There's no point in replacing one negative thought with another.

Sometimes all it takes is a single thought

Eileen Mulligan made a fortune in the beauty industry, then a back injury left her disabled and bedridden just as a serious dispute broke out which threatened to cripple her business.

She says, 'It looked like I had to have spinal surgery, *and* I wondered how I was going to survive the next six weeks. I realised I wasn't going to naturally wake up full of happy thoughts, but I did think if I could change the way I feel without changing my circumstances, just my thought processes, what could I do when I was back on my feet? So I concentrated on this. And I did it.'

It made all the difference. Eileen quit the business rather than continue the battle, and became a personal development coach. She has been so successful that her book, *Life Coaching*, is a bestseller and her clients include a number of well-known politicians and celebrities. The turning point? A change in her way of thinking!

10 Affirmations

It's time to consider **_affirmations_** in more detail.

Affirmations are a form of self-suggestion – a kind of sound-byte you give to yourself. They work on a principle known to advertisers and spin doctors the world over – repetition. If you tell someone, including yourself, something often enough, sooner or later you will be believed. The more skilful the phrasing of the message and the more forcefully expressed, the better.

Affirmations help to:

- _Emphasise_ your good points.
- _Change_ weaknesses into strengths.
- _Change_ attitudes.
- _Focus_ on what you want for yourself.

Affirmations are extremely effective in changing thinking patterns and programming the subconscious mind. With practice they become a powerful weapon in your confidence-building arsenal.

When we change our attitude towards ourselves, everything else changes as well, for our life is a reflection of the way we feel inside.

Dr Mansukh Patel

64 Start your affirmations with the first person pronoun, 'I'. For example:
'I accept, love and approve of myself and others.'
'I'm OK. I like myself. I'm proud to be me.'
'I am influenced only by confident thoughts and positive people.'
'I respect and admire myself.'

65 Use only positive words and phrases which describe what you want, rather than what you don't want. For example, say, 'I'm *confident*' rather than 'I am not shy', and 'I can *succeed*' rather than 'I will not *fail*.'

66 Make your affirmations credible. You won't leap from no confidence to perfect confidence overnight, so affirm your *willingness* and *determination* to change, and your *intention* to take the necessary steps. And – this is very important – put all personal weaknesses and limitations in the past tense.

A useful sentence construction is, 'I used to be... but all that is changing. Now I am becoming more and more... every day.'

Use this form of wording to compose an affirmation that is relevant to your current needs. For example, 'I used to be *shy*, but all that is changing. I am becoming more and more *sociable* every day. I am doing my best, and I know I will continue to improve.'

67 Writing down your affirmations reinforces them in the subconscious.

- Copy them out every day in CAPITAL LETTERS (this makes a greater impact on the subconscious).

- Jot them down in your diary and cheque book as a reminder.

- Write them on sticky labels and post them in prominent places around your home and in your car.

- Write them on small cards to carry with you and read throughout the day.

- Pin them to your Wall of Confidence.

68 Say your affirmations *as if you really mean them*. Aloud is best, although silently, under your breath, works well too. You never forget a thought expressed with strong emotion.

If a small voice in your head pipes up, 'You're lying, you know that's not true', remind yourself that this is merely your old programming. Tell it firmly to be quiet and go away.

69 Repeat each affirmation at least ten times, three or more times a day. The more you repeat them, the more effective they'll be. If possible look at yourself in the mirror as you recite them. Also, before you go to sleep run your favourite affirmations through in your mind, like a hypnotist.

70 Update your current list of affirmations regularly and keep it with you at all times. When one is no longer relevant, drop it and replace it with another.

Harness the power of suggestion

Suggestions, especially if made by someone in authority, can have enormous impact.

For example, every doctor knows that pills and potions with no active ingredients (placebos) can bring relief as long as the patient *believes* they can.

I once had a client who was terrified of flying. He told me his fear had been alleviated for a while by pills prescribed by his doctor that made him sleepy during the flight, but over time the effects wore off. When he mentioned this the doctor said he wasn't altogether surprised since they contained no active ingredients. With this knowledge the symptoms returned worse than before.

Use this power for yourself. Give yourself suggestions – lots of them. Do it often, since repetition is the key to success. Constantly tell yourself that you *value yourself*, you are worthy of *happiness*, you can *accomplish* anything you want, and you are *accepted* and *respected* by others.

11 Who do you *imagine* yourself to be?

Our imagination will stretch to any scenario, but people lacking in confidence usually *imagine* themselves as failures. They do not realise that they cannot succeed at anything if they cannot imagine themselves doing so.

How you imagine yourself may bear no relation to the truth, but it is this, rather than the reality, which governs your feelings and behaviour. Changing what you imagine about yourself can bring about a profound growth in confidence. When you *imagine* yourself as a good, capable, confident person, it becomes easier to *think* and *behave* like one.

Imagination is one of the cornerstones of the 1TIA Formula©. To understand why it is so important we must consider the subconscious mind in more detail. The mind is often compared to an iceberg, with more than 90% floating below the surface. This hidden mass is the **subconscious**, a vast storehouse of thoughts, memories and ideas.

The subconscious is always listening, watching, soaking up your experiences like a sponge. It then acts as a kind of database to which you constantly refer for guidance and support. Once your subconscious has accepted the idea that you are confident it makes sure your thinking, feelings and behaviour are brought into line; *it makes confidence your reality.*

You can talk to your subconscious, but it responds even better to mental images and emotions. Use your wonderful imagination to build confidence, by feeling and imagining yourself as confident until it becomes a natural part of you.

To come from no voice, no power, and to be able to achieve what I have means that only my own personal vision holds me back.

Oprah Winfrey

71 *Commit yourself* to spending a few minutes every day imagining yourself as you would like to be. This practice is called *Creative Imagery*. Either deliberately relax and calm your mind, or use those naturally occurring moments when you are relaxed. The longer and more vividly you can hold on to thoughts, feelings and mental images of yourself as a confident person when your mind is calm, the better.

72 Start by imagining something familiar, like an orange, a freshly baked loaf of bread, your house, a loved one, or a rose. Imagine the appearance, texture, taste and smell. Listen to a favourite piece of music, and imagine you can see the artist(s) performing it. Imagine the voice of a loved one.

Simple exercises such as these will bring about a rapid improvement in your creative imagery skills.

73 Creative imagery is often referred to as *visualisation*, which is slightly misleading because it is not strictly necessary to be able to make detailed pictures. All five senses, sight, touch/feel, sound, taste and smell – make an impact on the subconscious, especially when you're relaxed. So don't be put off if you can't actually 'see' anything: *feeling* a desire coming true is more important than getting a clear picture.

Take what you used yesterday. Now try to visualise it with all five senses. If you can't actually picture it, make more use of other senses.

74 Sit or lie comfortably, take a deep breath and close your eyes. Imagine yourself lying on a beautiful beach on a lovely summer's day. Picture the scene if you can. Imagine the sound of the sea, the warmth of the sun on your face, the softness of the sand, the smell of seaweed, and the feeling that you are safe and secure.

Practise, but don't force this exercise. The point is to use those senses with which you are most comfortable.

75 Whilst you are imagining relaxing on the beach, think of something you would like to achieve. Imagine or 'visualise' yourself as:

1. A confident person. Sense what it would feel like to be loaded with confidence.

2. Taking action. Feel yourself confidently pursuing your goal.

3. Having achieved everything for which you set out.

76 When you've mastered the above procedure, add a fourth stage:

4. 'Visualise' how you would like others to react towards you when you've accomplished your goal.

77 Use this affirmation:
'Every day I *see* myself as a confident person and I *feel* myself becoming more more confident.'

When willpower conflicts with the imagination, imagination prevails. Always.

David Lawrence Preston

The perfect shot

Many top sportsmen and women use creative imagery and mental rehearsal as an integral part of their mental toughness training. They know that when positive images are impressed firmly on the subconscious they're more likely to perform at their best. They spend many hours 'seeing' themselves hitting the perfect shot, throwing the javelin or discus further, crossing the winning line ahead of the competition, scoring goals and so on.

Pioneering the use of creative imagery in sport were professional golfers such as Jack Nicklaus and Arnold Palmer in the 1960s. At his peak Nicklaus said:

> 'I never hit a shot without having a sharp picture of it in
> my head. Firstly, I see where I want the ball to finish.
> Then I see it going there, its trajectory and landing.
> The next scene shows me making the swing that will turn
> the previous images into reality.'

12 Getting the most from creative imagery

To reiterate, creative imagery is the process of consciously creating a mental image or impression as a means of influencing the all-important subconscious mind. This section will help you get the most out of these techniques.

Techniques for creative imagery are best used when the body is relaxed and the mind is calm (see Section 25). They are also effective whenever you feel naturally dreamy, such as first thing in the morning, last thing at night and when daydreaming, because the mind is in a natural state of heightened awareness at these times.

Fantasising is good for you – do it often. Fantasise about all the things you want out of life, places to visit, people you would like to meet, acquiring new skills and being the person you would like to be. Let your imagination run wild!

First I dream my painting. Then I paint my dream.

Vincent Van Gogh

78 Be clear on what you would like to change or reinforce before you start, and choose feelings and images that symbolise your goal. For example, what does being confident mean to you? What do confident people look like? How do they move and speak? What do they do that makes them different from the rest?

79 Get your mind and body into a calm and relaxed state and use all five senses as much as possible to *imagine what you want as already yours*, happening right now, and working out *perfectly*.

For example, if you're rehearsing to go on stage, imagine you're looking out at the audience, enjoying the applause. Once you've imprinted this, your subconscious will do everything it can to make it come true for you.

80 Place the images in the centre of your mental screen. See everything in three dimensions using colour, brightness and movement, viewed as you would through your own senses, not as an onlooker. 'Hear' the sounds, 'smell' the smells with vivid clarity, and bring as much feeling into it as you can.

Remember, it is always more important to *feel* the desire coming true than to get the precise details of the visualisation clear.

81 Be gentle with yourself when using creative imagery, and don't force it. Too much effort is self-defeating. Just allow the sounds, images and sensations to materialise.

82 Reinforce creative imagery with ***autosuggestion.*** This is the use of positive self-talk and affirmations when the subconscious is relaxed and receptive.

Here's a powerful autosuggestive technique. Either memorise these words, or record them onto a cassette tape. Repeat them, or listen to the tape, every night just before you go to sleep, and when you wake up in the morning. Say the words quietly to yourself as you listen.

'I, (your name), am a very confident person.'
'You, (your name), are a very confident person.'
'(Your name) is a very confident person.'

83 Practise mental rehearsal. If you know you're going to face a difficult challenge, spend a few minutes each day imagining yourself there, thinking and acting confidently. Imagine it as if it were already happening and working out perfectly. The more you mentally rehearse, the more you'll be at your best and handle it with ease when the time comes.

84 Use creative imagery frequently. Short daily sessions are more effective than lengthy but infrequent ones. If you don't see immediate results, be patient. Don't give up. You may be dissolving emotional blockages that have been there for years.

Calm, confident and in control

Vicky came to see me several years ago. She had applied to take a motorcycle test, and although she was a competent car driver and felt confident she could ride a motorcycle perfectly well, she was terrified of the actual test. On previous occasions, she had gone to pieces on the day.

I taught her to enter a deeply relaxed state and visualise herself taking the test with total confidence. Vicky found it easy to make mental pictures and had no problem imagining herself looking over the handlebars, feeling the vibration through the seat of her pants, hearing the sound of the engine, smelling the oil and exhaust fumes. She also used autosuggestion: 'I am calm, confident and in control.'

Then she visualised the examiner congratulating her on her success. She conjured up feelings of pride, happiness and excitement as he handed her the pass slip. Finally she visualised herself arriving home to an ecstatic welcome from her husband, who took her out for a celebration meal.

Vicky practised every day. Two weeks later I went on holiday. On my return I found a postcard on the mat. It said in gold lettering, 'I was calm, I was confident, I was in control, and I passed! Can't believe how well it worked. Many thanks.'

13 The 'As If' Principle

When a young man enlists in the army he is made to conduct himself like a soldier from day one. The army knows that this way he will quickly *feel like* a soldier and *become* one.

Similarly, when you speak and act confidently – even if it's all a pretence – you feel more confident. Others assume you're confident and treat you accordingly, which reinforces your behaviour and makes you feel even more confident.

The opposite is also true. If you speak and act timidly, others assume you are timid and treat you as such, which reinforces your timidity.

The 'As If' Principle is the fourth element of the ITIA Formula©. It simply states that when you act *as if* you are confident, no matter how uncomfortable you feel inside, you *become* confident. Your feelings soon adapt to the new behaviour and, if you persevere, confidence blooms.

Assume a virtue if you have it not.

William Shakespeare

85

In your notebook describe how you would behave and what you would do if you were confident.

Now do it. Behave that way.

86

People can be full of confidence on the *outside* but plagued with self-doubt *inside*. Make a list of well-known people, alive or deceased, who seem, or seemed, confident, but admitted to lacking confidence. Add anyone you know, or knew, personally. How did they conceal their lack of confidence? What did they *do* to appear confident? If you're not sure, try to find out.

87

Use the ***Modelling*** technique. Modelling is based on the common sense notion that you can avoid a great deal of struggle and inconvenience by finding someone who is already confident, and learning from them.

Start by making a list of people you know, have heard of, read about or seen in films and on TV, whom you admire and would like to emulate. They could be, for instance, the most popular people at work or school, historical figures, or even fictional characters.

88

Pick two or three models from your list in Confidence Builder 87, and find out as much as you can about them. If you know them personally, quietly observe them; if not, read about them, hire films or videos and put yourself in their shoes. Imagine what it must be like to *be* these people.

Which of their qualities do you already possess? Which do you lack?

89 For one hour act as if you are one of your role models, and put what you've learned about them into practice. If you have access to video recording equipment, record and observe yourself and learn from it.

Gradually extend one hour to two, three... then an entire day. If it feels uncomfortable (and it probably will), remember that all change feels uncomfortable at first. Many confident people, including possibly your role models, had to work at it.

90 When you first apply the 'As If' Principle uncomfortable feelings will surface – you won't be able to prevent them. But don't let this stop you. Go ahead and do it anyway. In time you will no longer be affected by them.

91 Choose something you really enjoy or *know* you have a talent for, and become an expert in it. The confidence gained will radiate from you and do wonders for you in other areas too. Confidence thrives on itself. Nothing succeeds like success!

Be somebody. If you have lost confidence in yourself, make believe you are somebody else, somebody with brains, and act like him.

Sol Hess

'So unsure, I invented this character.'

Actor and heart-throb Roger Moore, best known for playing James Bond, developed his famous persona precisely because he was lacking in confidence as a young man. He was so overweight and shy his father called him 'a sack of shit tied up ugly in the middle'.

'I was so unsure of myself, I would rather starve than go into a restaurant,' he says. 'So I built a wall of defence and invented this character Roger Moore.'

Acting '*as if*' may be a little daunting at first, but remember, the anxiety is simply your subconscious trying to cling to old habits. Do it anyway, and it soon fades. Then the very same mechanism that once tried to stop you changing defends your new behaviour and will continue to do so until you try to make further changes.

14 Eat an elephant

How do you eat an elephant? One bite at a time. How do you climb a ladder? One rung at a time. How do you build confidence? One step at a time.

When you take small steps, the anxiety you inevitably feel is more manageable. That's why it's important to have a go at things which you would previously have found scary on a regular basis. Do you find it hard to talk to people? Strike up a conversation with one new person every day! Do you keep quiet even when you have something to say? Speak up, say your piece! You gain encouragement and feel more confident every time you build on each small success.

Don't let uncomfortable feelings stop you, they come partly from your subconscious programming and partly from what you tell yourself about the situation. Stay calm, change the self-talk (using the Four Step Method), and persevere.

Remember, courage is not the absence of fear, but *ignoring fear* and proceeding in spite of it.

Try a thing you haven't tried before three times: once to get over the fear, once to find out how to do it, and a third time to find out if you like it or not.

Virgil Thomson

92 Do something practical to expand your self-confidence every day. Take measured risks. Each small step should be accompanied by a clear intention, an affirmation (or change of thinking) and mental rehearsal.

93 Make a list of any habits, mannerisms, modes of speech or behaviours which give away your lack of confidence.

Add the elimination of these to the goals you set for yourself in Section 5. Grade your goals according to (1) importance and (2) difficulty.

94 Work backwards from each goal and break it down into small steps. Establish a challenging but realistic schedule for completing each step. Set deadlines. Write them in your diary and notebook.

95 Adopt the Boy Scouts' motto, 'Be prepared'. Before taking each step, do your homework. Find out what you need to do, practise the skills and acquire the relevant knowledge. Ninety per cent of the outcome in any activity depends on the quality of the preparation undertaken.

96
As you tackle each step, use the full ITIA Formula©. Use an affirmation such as:

I am confident, enthusiastic and fully capable of... (name the step you are about to take).

97
Mentally rehearse each step. Imagine it done well and 'see' it working out perfectly.

98
Now go ahead and do it! Ignore any anxiety or discomfort, and remind yourself that anything your mind can conceive and believe, you can achieve. If it doesn't work out, change your approach if necessary, and try again.

Above all, keep your mind on what you want, never lose sight of your goal, and persevere.

You now have all the basic tools and techniques for building your confidence and self-esteem.

Keep practising them while you proceed to the next few sections. (We'll revisit some of them later in more detail.) Meanwhile, we move on to the essential area of *self-awareness*.

Knowing yourself is a cornerstone of all personal growth. It's hard to change anything, including yourself, without understanding how it is now. All I ask is that you undertake the exercises with truthfulness and sincerity.

You may try to hide certain aspects of yourself from others, but there's no point in hiding them from yourself if you want to make genuine progress.

To grow in confidence

> **Clarify** your intention and set goals.
> **Train** yourself to think more confidently.
> **Imagine** yourself as confident.
> **Act** as if you are confident.

> ### *Plus*

> **Develop greater self-awareness.**

15 Self-Awareness 1: Your past

Everything is a result of what's gone before. Your level of confidence is mainly the result of the way you responded to those who raised you and the environment in which you grew up. But it is not the whole story.

Genetics – **nature** – accounts for around 25-35% of your character. Your past experiences and your interpretation of them – **nurture** – the remainder. When you were born you didn't lack confidence – this came later, when you began to relate to other people and the world around you.

Confidence, or lack of it, is *learned*, mostly in the first few years of childhood. It developed when you were weak and mentally and emotionally vulnerable, then, as you grew up, it became self-reinforcing. So the better you understand what happened and how it affected you, the more effectively you can take charge of your present-day feelings and actions.

You may find that some of the exercises in the next few sections bring painful feelings to the surface, but don't be deterred. Be honest with yourself. You gain nothing by deliberately misleading or deceiving yourself.

Knowing others is intelligence.
Knowing yourself is true wisdom.
Mastering others is strength.
Mastering yourself is true power.

Lao Tsu

99 Write your life story, picking out significant events and episodes that most affected your confidence. No need to write a novel – just a few notes will do fine.

100 Sit quietly and reflect on your life.

- What are the main difficulties, losses and setbacks that you remember?

- How did you cope?

- Do you still have any feelings about those events?

- Are there any regrets?

- What strengths and resources have these hardships and losses given you?

- How often has your confidence let you down? In what way?

101 What were your biggest mistakes? Your biggest failures? How did they affect you *then*? How do they affect you *now*?

102 Of what are you most ashamed? Do you have any guilty secrets, anything you would not want anyone else to discover about your past?

103 Write down this sentence:

The most incredible thing I've ever done is...

Quickly, without thinking about it too hard, write down the first six things that come to mind. You see, you've had your moments. Acknowledge *all* your past achievements, however trivial they seem.

104 This exercise is best done when you are in a relaxed frame of mind. Let your thoughts wander back to a time when you felt really confident (everyone has *at least* one). Where were you, and with whom? What happened? Run the events through in your mind – 'see', 'hear', 'feel', *relive* them as if they were happening all over again.

You don't necessarily have to *imagine* what it's like to be confident. You already know!

105 Which of these phrases best describes how you feel about your childhood?

- I had a very happy childhood.

- My childhood was quite happy.

- It was OK, neither happy nor unhappy.

- My childhood was not very happy.

- I had a miserable childhood.

Why did you choose that particular phrase?

One day I finally realised I no longer needed a personal history – so I gave it up.

Carlos Castaneda

16 Self-awareness 2: What are you like?

Confidence and self-esteem do not come in fixed amounts – they vary from place to place, moment to moment according to what you're doing and with whom. For example, some people are extremely confident at work but fail in their relationships; and many brilliant individuals can barely string two words together when away from the security of their offices or laboratories.

How about you?

Take a close look at yourself. *Step back and observe*. The more self-aware you are, the more control you have over your life.

Then, and only then, is lasting change possible.

Know yourself, know your enemy,
A hundred battles, a hundred victories.

Mao Tse-Tung

106 For one week jot down every negative reaction towards yourself in your notebook. Include all self-criticisms and put downs (spoken and unspoken), self-defeating and self-sabotaging behaviour, and so on. Write them down as soon as you can.

Look at what you've written. What can you learn from it?

107 Every day for one week spend 20 minutes in quiet contemplation, getting in touch with your inner self. Sit or lie comfortably, take a deep breath and close your eyes. Focus your attention on what's going on inside you: bodily sensations, thoughts, emotional feelings, mental images and daydreams. If possible vary these sessions by time of day – morning, midday, afternoon and evening to allow for the fact that moods and feelings fluctuate throughout the day.

Immediately after each session write down whatever comes to mind.

108 Write down these sentences and fill in the gaps:
'I lack the confidence to..., but now I know I can overcome my doubts.'
'I get anxious when..., but now I know I can conquer my fears.'
Take each in turn and quickly write down the first six things that enter your head.

109 Think about your talents, skills and abilities.

1. How capable do you feel of achieving *anything* you set your mind to?

2. In which situations do you feel most competent? Least competent?

3. How competent do you feel in your work/career/academic endeavours?

4. How capable do you feel of being successful in your leisure and sporting activities?

5. Do you ever begrudge others their success?

6. Do you tend to over-dramatise or makes mountains out of molehills?

110 Think about your personal relationships:

1. How well do you manage your intimate relationships? Your family life? Friendships?

2. How comfortable are you in social situations, e.g. parties, social events at work, wedding receptions, etc?

3. Are you ever accused of being boastful or pretentious?

4. Do you usually prefer to stay in the background?

5. Do you ever feel uncomfortable because you think everyone's looking at you?

6. Do you give way easily when someone disagrees with you?

7. Do you find it difficult to say no when you want to?

8. Do you take decisions based on your own instincts or allow others to push you around?

9. Are you living the way you choose, or doing mainly what others think you should?

10. If you answered no to question 9, why do you think this is?

111 Think about your self-esteem/self-worth:

1. Do you often feel sorry for yourself?

2. Do you tend to blame yourself when things go wrong, even if circumstances are beyond your control?

3. Do you frequently criticise others?

4. Do you frequently criticise yourself?

5. Do you take good care of your health and fitness?

6. Do you believe you have to achieve great things before you can feel good about yourself?

7. Do you have a tendency to go to pieces when someone criticises you?

8. Do you go out of your way to seek approval from others?

9. Are you comfortable with the notion of a spiritual dimension to life?

10. Are you generally happy?

112 When you look in the mirror, are you proud to be the person you see?

If the answer is no, write down what you would have to do or become before you *could* be proud of who you are.

17 Childhood

Your self-image began to take shape even before you left the cradle and was pretty well established by the time you reached the age of 8.

By then, on average, you had already received over 70,000 negative dictates: 'Don't do that', 'No you can't', 'Who do you think you are?' 'You'll never make anything of yourself,' and so on. Most of these were run of the mill reprimands to which adults attach little importance; but they affect a child deeply and the accumulated effect can be devastating. The truth is, *children simply do not have the ability to distinguish between fair and unfair criticism, or make allowances if the adults in their lives have had a hard day.*

When you pleased your parents, or other adult authority figures, they rewarded you: they gave you attention and approval. When you displeased them, they showed their disapproval by withdrawing attention or privileges or, in some cases, punishing you physically. The means by which a person moulds the behaviour of another using a combination of reward and punishment is termed **conditioning**. You experienced plenty of it as a child, much of it negative. Very few young people reach adulthood without having their confidence dented in some way.

Once you understand your conditioning you can unravel the knots, dispense with the ropes that tied you down and leave them behind forever.

Children begin by loving their parents.
After a time they judge them.
Rarely, if ever, do they forgive them.

Oscar Wilde

113

Many people believe that it is impossible to overcome negative conditioning, but this is simply not true. Many highly successful people suffered difficulties as children. For instance, a recent survey discovered that 90% of the chief executives of the UK's top companies lost a parent through death or divorce before the age of 16. All claimed that, instead of destroying them, it strengthened their determination to succeed.

What happened to you in childhood did not determine your level of confidence, *but your attitude to it.*

Think of a childhood incident which you always believed damaged your self-confidence. How would taking a different attitude help?

114

Write down this sentence:
'My mother's opinion of me made me believe that...'
Quickly, without thinking about it too hard, write down the first few thoughts that come into your head.

115

Write down this sentence:
'My father's opinion of me made me believe that...'
Again without thinking about it too hard, quickly write down the first thoughts that come into your head.

116

Parents' and teachers' words and sayings can stick in the mind for many years.

For example a recent client, now in his 50s, told me he still hears his mother's words ringing in his ears: 'Life's a bitch, and then you die!' Another told me how his father drummed into him, 'When you can choose the hard way or the easy way son, do it the hard way. It builds character.' The poor man had spent a lifetime making things more complicated than they need have been.

What parental expressions do you recall from your childhood? How strong an impression did they make on you? How do you feel when you think about them now?

117

When were your parents or guardians most proud of you? When were they least proud? How has this affected you?

When (if they are still living) are they most proud of you nowadays? When are they least proud? How does this affect you today?

118

Where did helping you to build your confidence and self-esteem rank on your parents' or guardians' list of priorities? Did they praise you often? Criticise constructively? Were they generous with their time? Or preoccupied with other things, like enforcing the house rules or pursuing their own interests?

Make notes on how this affected you.

119

Were you brought up in a particular religion? What did it teach you about yourself? Did it make you feel strong, capable and secure, or a hopeless, worthless sinner?

'The boy's got to learn to be a man'

Sir John Harvey Jones is the very model of a successful businessman. Now in his mid 70s, the former Chairman of ICI (once Britain's largest company) looks back on a brilliant career as a Royal Navy Officer, highly respected entrepreneur, and lately writer and broadcaster. Yet his early years were hardly auspicious and as a boy he didn't see his father for 20 years!

Born in India, he was sent away to boarding school at the age of 6. 'I was bullied mercilessly,' he recalls. 'The bullying was both physical and verbal, and always with numbers, never one-on-one. It resulted in my trying to slash my wrists in the toilet with a blunt penknife.'

'Everybody knew I was dreadfully unhappy. I'd written to my parents and told them I was desperate, but I figure my father thought the boy's got to learn to be a man and stand up for himself.'

At 12, he left the school to go to Naval College, which he describes as 'Pretty draconian. The discipline was horrendous.'

One of the best days of his life was seeing his old school bulldozed to the ground prior to redevelopment. Like many successful people who suffered abuse in childhood, it's not that he has forgotten what happened – the memories are crystal clear. It's that he simply decided not to let it hold him back.

18 Control dramas

In his best-selling book, *The Celestine Prophecy*, James Redfield suggests that adults go about attracting the love, recognition, approval and support they need according to the kind of interactions they had with their parents as children. We learned how to attract attention from them, and continued to play these dramas over and over again, usually subconsciously, until they became habitual. Unless we become aware of them and make a conscious effort to change, they stay with us for life.

Redfield suggests that these control dramas come in four types. Most of us have a favoured style, and adopt others from time to time according to circumstances:

- **Intimidator**
- **Interrogator**
- **Aloof**
- **Poor me**

Understanding control dramas is extremely helpful. Once you have decided into which group you, your parents/guardians, siblings and anyone else who had a profound impact on your childhood fit most comfortably, you can use these insights to develop greater understanding of your childhood conditioning, and yourself as you are now.

No matter what kind of journey we make of life,
where we started out will always be part of us.
But only part.

Sir Alex Ferguson

---

120 Divide a piece of paper into four quadrants, one for each control drama: **intimidator, interrogator, aloof,** and **poor me**.

Think of the influential adults in your early life. If any of these tried to control you by being loud, aggressive or physically threatening, list them under 'Intimidators'.

Note: (a) If either parent was an intimidator, the chances are the other was either also an intimidator or a poor me. (b) Intimidators tend to create poor me children.

---

121 **Interrogators** are less *physically* threatening; they break down resistance by making sarcastic, derogatory comments, asking probing questions and finding fault: 'Who do you think you are?' 'Why didn't you?' 'I told you so', etc. Interrogators can be cynical, arrogant and self-righteous.

Note: intimidators create aloof children and sometimes poor me's, both seeking to escape from constant scrutiny. Were either of your parents an interrogator?

---

122 **Aloofs** enjoy attention and approval as much as anyone, but employ quite a different strategy. Often reserved, they believe that others will try to draw them out if they create an aura of mystery and intrigue: 'You don't know what I'm really thinking and feeling.' They don't realise their aloofness may actually prevent them from getting attention, because the more they back off, the more unapproachable they seem.

Note: Aloofs usually create interrogator children. Were either of your parents an aloof?

123 **Poor me** people feel too powerless to take on the world actively, so they seek sympathy by playing the victim. They wear worried expressions and relate tales of tragedy and personal crisis, often accompanied by deep sighing and sobbing. They may try the aloof, silent treatment, but make sure that it is noticed. Another favoured tactic is the guilt trip: 'If you really loved me, you'd...' 'Look at what you're doing to me.' 'Please don t hurt me, I'm so weak.'

Note: Poor me people often sustain their victim-stance by subconsciously seeking out people who abuse them. For example, a poor me wife may attract an intimidator husband. The pay-off is the intimidator's apology and remorse – which, however, is usually false and short-term. Were either of your parents a poor me person?

124 Which of the four control drama types best describes you?

- Are you the angry, impatient type? Do you attempt to dominate others?

- Do you enjoy needling or interrogating people?

- Do you like to keep your distance and play hard to get?

- Or do you enjoy feeling sorry for yourself, worrying, complaining and focusing on problems?

125 If you' re still not clear into which group you belong, think about what happened if you disagreed with your parents/guardians. What happened if you disobeyed them? What happens if you disagree with them or ignore their wishes now?

126 What types do you attract nowadays? Stop matching their dramas.

For instance, practise using assertive words and phrases in the presence of intimidators, and politely but firmly let poor me people know you will no longer pander to their self-pitying claptrap. And if you find yourself indulging in self-pity, stop immediately.

'I can't but I have to'

One of the most damaging patterns of negative conditioning arises when children are continually told or given the impression by intimidator or interrogator adults that they're no good, they'll never make anything of themselves. 'You do that? Don't make me laugh!'

Children subjected to this kind of talk grow up with no confidence and often terrified of failure.

It's even worse if they are victims of conditional love – when it is made clear, explicitly or implicitly, that they will only be loved if they meet the adults' expectations: 'Do this – or else!' This often produces an obsession with what other people think and winning their approval.

Worst of all is the double negative self-talk which torments an individual who, because of their conditioning, feels driven to perform but is too afraid to try: 'I can't but I have to' is a common aloof or poor me pattern which probably accounts for most of the failure these unfortunates experience as adults.

19 Take care of your Inner Child

The child you once were lives on inside you, influencing every thought, every emotion, every move. You're with each other every minute of the day.

Many people are in adult bodies but they still react like children, still attached to their parents, never having broken free from the attitudes and beliefs they acquired in their youth.

Your Inner Child is the part of your personality which:

- Is playful and spontaneous
- Likes having fun
- Is imaginative
- Loves the world of 'let's pretend'
- Is sensitive
- Needs to be cared for and understood
- Likes to please, seeking love and approval in return.

Like a real child, an Inner Child starved of love, warmth and understanding is easily hurt, and may become depressed and withdrawn.

The Inner Child can be the source of much adult unhappiness if it is still harbouring anger, pain and guilt from earlier years. If this is true for you, you can never be truly confident and happy unless these feelings are resolved.

Learn to accept your Inner Child as an important and valuable part of you.

Whatever our upbringing has been, as adults our self-esteem is in our own hands.

Dr Nathaniel Branden

127 Place a photograph of yourself as a child in a prominent place, such as on your Wall of Confidence. Smile and acknowledge it every day. Talk to him or her, tell him you love and will take care of him.

128 Most small children feel hurt and vulnerable at one time or another. Similarly everyone feels like a child at times, innocent and in need of tenderness and care.

To what extent do you acknowledge these aspects of yourself? Do you comfort your Inner Child sufficiently when she or he feels lost and lonely, helpless or upset?

Imagine her sat on your knee, enjoying a few intimate moments. How do you feel? Promise to be less hard on this part of yourself in future.

129 If you were to listen to your Inner Child, what do you think he or she would say?

Try the empty chair technique. Take two chairs and position them facing each other. Sit on one, and imagine yourself as a small child on the other. Talk to each other. Ask how he feels about the way you treat him. Say how you feel about him. Then switch seats and *be* him, responding to 'you'. Keep switching chairs, and try to gain a greater understanding of each other.

130

That little person couldn't help being vulnerable, shy, timid, unworldly and, yes, childish. So even though strictly speaking there's nothing to forgive, write the following sentences in your notebook and fill the gaps with the first thoughts that come into your head:

'Now I can forgive that I was... as a child. I can forgive myself for what I couldn't do and couldn't cope with, including...'

131

To what extent do you still allow your parents/guardians to control your thoughts, words and actions *now*? What changes would you like to make?

Use the ITIA Formula© to put them into practice.

- State what *you intend* to change.

- Bring your *thoughts* into line.

- *Imagine* the change as if already made.

- *Act as if* change is already happening and is inevitable.

132

Have more fun. Make a point of being more playful. Every day do more of those silly things that you enjoyed as a child. Look for the funny side in every situation. Your Inner Child will experience real enjoyment.

133

Take up a hobby that requires you to be more imaginative – painting and drawing, making music, creative writing, a favourite craft, acting, dancing etc. Remember, your Inner Child loves using her imagination and, of course, imagination is one of the cornerstones of the ITIA Formula©.

'Her fault, not mine'

Celia believed she had been unloved as a child. Her father abandoned his wife and daughter soon after she was born, and her mother was always busy. She remembered feeling alone and pleading with her mother to play with her, but Mum always shooed her away. 'I always felt it was my fault,' she said. 'I must have been really boring.'

In therapy Celia entered the relaxed state and pictured herself as a child. She imagined the little girl she once was sat on her knee, being comforted. They chatted to each other; the little girl insisted that she was not boring, just lonely. She hated the way she was recollected by the adult Celia. She considered it very unfair. As she visualised herself enjoying a warm, lingering cuddle, tears welled up.

The following week Celia felt much better about her childhood and herself. 'I now realise I was oK,' she said. 'If my mother didn't want to know, that was her fault, not mine.'

Like Celia you will only be able to accept your Inner Child as an important and valuable part of you when you stop judging him or her and treat her with compassion instead.

20 Forgive, forget and be free

No matter how you feel about it, as an adult you are totally responsible for the way you respond to everything that happens. Thinking otherwise just keeps you stuck in a victim pattern. *Confidence and inner peace will only be yours when you stop blaming and practise forgiveness.*

Who is there to forgive? Anyone whom you have ever blamed for how your life has turned out including, of course, your parents or guardians. After all, they had parents too! They were products of their own conditioning. They too may have suffered from low self-esteem or been under stress, and if they hurt you it was probably because they didn't know any better.

Besides, forgiveness doesn't mean *condoning* what was done, only that you are willing to live with whatever happened. And whether the perpetrators deserve to be forgiven is irrelevant; they may be completely culpable.

But you don't do it for *them*. You do it for *yourself.*

You're only hurting yourself by hanging on to the bitterness and resentment you've been carrying around with you.

Forgiveness is not necessarily easy, but is absolutely essential if you are to grow in maturity, self-esteem and confidence. It's how you set yourself free.

If you haven't forgiven your parents,
you haven't left home.

Anon.

---

134 If you catch yourself blaming anyone else for the way you are now, say 'Stop!' and repeat the following affirmations until the blaming thoughts have gone away:

'I, and no one else, am in charge of my life.'
'From now on I no longer blame anyone else for anything
I dislike about myself.'

---

135 Make a list of all the people who have hurt you, let you down, lied or cheated on you in the past. If possible find a photograph of them. Beside each name write down why you included them.

---

136 Review your list. As you contemplate each name, look at their photo or make an image of them in your mind. Really *feel* your hurt and/or anger. Then, whatever they did to you, or you imagine they did to you, let it go. Say with sincerity, 'I forgive you. From now on I send only love.'

---

137 Imagine your father or male parent figure in the Empty Chair (see Confidence Builder 129). Tell him everything you've withheld from him down the years – resentments, frustrations, etc. Then switch seats and be him, responding to you, and keep switching chairs until you've exhausted the discussion.

138 Do the same with your mother or female parent figure.

When you use the Empty Chair technique, remember: (1) It is not a rehearsal for a real life encounter; the other person may even no longer be alive. It is a way of clearing unexpressed feelings that keep you stuck in the past. (2) Most of us don't remember our parents as they *actually* were, but as we *think* or *imagine* they were.

139 If you can't find room for forgiveness in your heart at present, affirm the possibility that one day, perhaps sooner than you think, you could be ready to forgive. This affirmation sends a powerful message to the subconscious:

'Soon, I will be ready to forgive... (name him or her) for...
(whatever they did)
and wipe the slate clean. I, and I alone, am in charge of my life.'

140 Don't forget to forgive the most important person in your life – you. Forgive yourself for all your failings; for being too hard on yourself; for sometimes failing to stand up for yourself; and for any hurt you've caused to others.

If you were wrong or made a mistake, stop dwelling on it. Learn from the experience and move on.

'From this day on, I send you love'

Dr Wayne Dyer's first book, *Your Erroneous Zones* has sold over 35 million copies, and subsequent works, including *Pulling Your Own Strings*, *Real Magic* and *The Sky's The Limit* have inspired millions more. He speaks to packed auditoriums all over the world. Yet it was not always so. In his early 30s, he was far from successful, two stones overweight, trapped in an unhappy relationship and, by his own admission, a candidate for an early heart attack.

Dr Dyer points to one specific incident as the turning point in his life – an act of forgiveness. When he was a baby his father, a man with a reputation as wifebeater, alcoholic and petty criminal, walked out, never to make contact again. He died at a relatively young age. Dr Dyer had grown to detest him and frequently had nightmares about beating him up.

Then, in 1974, he found himself at his father's grave, angrily demanding an explanation. Suddenly, something came over him. The hurt and hatred melted away and he offered a prayer: 'From this day on, I send you love.' Then he walked away.

Immediately, everything changed. Within two weeks, he wrote *Your Erroneous Zones*. He started exercising (now 60, he claims to have run at least eight miles every day since), terminated the painful relationship and forged a reputation that is second to none in his field.

Ask him about his past, he shrugs his shoulders. 'It happened,' he says. 'That's all.'

21 Let go of the past

The past lives on only in your thoughts. It is dead, but *you're not*. You'll grow in confidence only if you are willing to let go of the past, learn from it, and move on.

No matter what has gone before, your future, and how you feel about it, will be a direct result of what you do from now on. It is being shaped right now, moment by moment, as the consequences of your desires, thoughts, dreams, actions and words begin to crystallise.

The past only continues to affect you if you allow it.

You may not be able to forget what has gone before, but you *can* stop dwelling on it.

You can't have a better tomorrow if you are thinking about yesterday all the time.

Charles F. Kettering

141 What 'baggage' are you still carrying from your past? Which, if any, of your negative experiences continue to haunt you?

Write a short paragraph on each, describing what happened, how they affected you, and why it's important to let go of them now you are an adult.

142 Stop *talking* about the past, especially mistakes and misfortunes. If you catch yourself breaking this rule, change the subject. *Immediately.* Stop portraying yourself as a 'poor me'.

143 If you find yourself dwelling on the past and feeling sorry for yourself, ask yourself the following and note any internal reactions – physical, mental or emotional:

- Am I sure I've got my facts straight?

- What else could this mean?

- What positive value does it have?

- What can I learn from it that will benefit me in the future?

144 Use this affirmation. Make it into a poster and display it on your Wall of Confidence:

'I am willing to release the past and live fully in the present.'

145 Master the *reframing* technique. Reframing is a way of changing how you feel about past events that still trouble you:

1. Relax your body. Still your thoughts.

2. Go back to an event which left its mark on you and get in touch with all the emotions you felt at the time.

3. Now reframe it. Run the scene through in your mind, but visualise a different outcome. 'See' it happening as you would have liked, really 'feel' it. With practice your mind will accept this as reality.

4. Over time you can work through as many 'difficult' memories as you wish. Start with the least troublesome then, as you become more proficient at using the technique, tackle more serious issues.

The reframing technique sends a powerful message to your subconscious to record over old tapes with new, more positive, confidence building interpretations of events.

146 Resolve from now on to focus your attention on what you've *achieved* in life and *intend* to achieve, not what you have *not* achieved. Use the Four Step Method to veto inappropriate thoughts.

147 Add this affirmation to your repertoire:

> 'I used to lack confidence, but all that is changing now.
> I am becoming more and more confident every day.'

'How dare he?'

Eric was 11 years old when the headmaster called him up to the front of the school and announced in front of everyone, 'Here is a worthless, stupid boy who will never make anything of himself'. The incident had dogged him for years. When I met him, he was 47 years old.

Under hypnosis he recalled the original incident. Tears streamed down his face. He then re-enacted the scene, but this time told the head very forcefully, 'Oh no I'm not! You're out of order. Apologise!' He imagined the headmaster on his knees in front of him, grovelling.

Now he smiles at the memory. 'The stupid man', he says. 'How dare he speak to me, or any other young person, like that?'

22 Self-acceptance

Self-acceptance means acknowledging that you are as you are and being comfortable with it. It doesn't necessarily mean *liking* every aspect of yourself.

Some attributes can't be changed, and you may as well accept them right now. Take your age. You can disguise it, lie about it, try to hide it, but you can't change it. Similarly, you can do little about your gender (without going to drastic lengths), your race, height, eye colour etc. You also have little chance of transforming the way the world works, society in general and other people. But you *can* find a way of making the best of yourself, by:

- becoming better informed
- acquiring new skills
- changing unwanted habits
- handling relationships and problems more effectively.

But bear in mind, *self-acceptance does not mean giving up on yourself.* If some disliked aspect of yourself is important and can be changed, do something about it. There's no point in feeling bad about something you can change, just as there's no point in feeling bad about something you *can't!*

Never grow old in your mind.
Your true age is how you feel inside.

Valerie J. Hayward

148 What aspects of yourself do you find most difficult to accept? Are there times or situations when you find it harder to be self-accepting than others? If you wish jot down what stops you giving yourself permission to be as you are.

149 Write down everything you *dislike* about yourself. Include anything at which you feel you're not particularly good. Be honest: but don't exaggerate or wallow in self-pity.

150 Go through your list (from Confidence Builder 149) and underline any things you dislike that *cannot* be changed. Then look again: are you sure there's nothing you can do to change them? Eliminate any which are merely the result of negative conditioning.

151 Use this affirmation:

'I accept my... and my... (the attributes you have underlined).
This is me, and I'm wonderful, aren't I?'

152

Do you ever feel that your best is never good enough?

If you judge yourself as not good enough, no amount of *achievement* will ever satisfy you. Ask yourself: 'How realistic are the goals and standards I set myself?'

There's a paradox here. There's nothing wrong with having *high* expectations of yourself: *low* expectations lead to underachievement. But *impossible* ones destroy your confidence.

153

Write down this sentence:

'When I fail to live up to my expectations or fall below the standards I set myself, I tell myself...'

Write down the first six thoughts that come into your head. Why are you so hard on yourself? You don't have to be perfect, you know.

154

Stop comparing yourself with others. You'll always find people who are better than you at some things, and people who are worse. The only meaningful comparison is between you as *you used to be*, and you *as you are now*. No one is better than anyone else, just different.

If you lapse into thinking 'I'm not as... (attractive/clever/athletic etc) as...', stop it. Tell yourself, 'I'm a wonderful, amazing being. I'm good enough, and I'm grateful for it.'

The moment you accept yourself as you are, all burdens, all mountainous burdens, simply disappear. Then life is a sheer joy, a festival of lights.

Osho

'A different kind of hearing.'

At the age of 11 Evelyn Glennie was told that she would have to attend a special school for the deaf. It was a moment that changed her life. She became determined to go to the local secondary school attended by her brothers.

'It didn't make sense that simply because a chart says you can't hear such and such, you therefore can't do certain things,' she said in a recent interview. With her parents' support she ignored the audiologist and went to the mainstream school anyway.

Now, despite being completely deaf since the age of 11, Evelyn is one of the world's top classical percussionists, feted all over the world, performing barefoot to help her feel vibrations from the other instruments. When asked how she copes with her hearing problem she replies that she doesn't 'see' herself as deaf – just someone with a different kind of hearing. Her other senses are enhanced and her concentration heightened: she simply 'listens' harder.

'I never asked, "Why me?"', she says. 'We've all got something that needs sorting. You meet people really handicapped who appear to be the happiest people in the world. That puts life in perspective.'

23 Body image

What do you think of your body? Do you like it? Do you wish it were different in some way? If so, it may surprise you to discover that you're in the great majority. Most of us don't particularly like our bodies and could produce a lengthy list of 'faults' quite easily. Few people conform to the physical norms put across in the media.

People who can't accept their bodies are prone to desperately low self-esteem. They exhibit an above average degree of obsessive behaviours, eating disorders, self-hatred, sexual dysfunctions and many other problems. This is exacerbated by certain social and religious attitudes.

Rumbling tummies, bad breath, bowel movements and breaking wind are part of our biology. Why be ashamed? When we get older our faces become lined, boobs and bellies droop, muscles sag, men lose their hair and so on. It's bound to happen, so why worry about it?

We must learn to accept our bodies with good grace and a touch of humour, to accept some of our so-called defects, and work on those which can be changed.

If your confidence is affected by anything that can be improved, do it! Otherwise there's no point in feeling sorry for yourself.

If we are embarrassed about our bodies, we should remember that kings and philosophers shit, and so do ladies.

Michel Montaigne

---

155 What do you think of your body shape and physical appearance?

Think about what you *like*. Focus your attention on these parts. Stand in front of a mirror, look yourself in the eye and say, 'I like myself, I really do.' Let your inner beauty shine through. Now do it naked. Notice how you feel.

---

156 Which parts of your body do you *dislike*?

Think about those you can do nothing about – your shoe size, the length of your legs, birth marks, etc. As you look at yourself in the mirror, acknowledge that this is how your body is and repeat the affirmation:

'This is me. I'm wonderful, aren't I?'

---

157 Now take the things about your body you *don't* like and which *can* be changed, for example excess weight, poor muscle tone, greying hair and smoking-related afflictions. Go through your list and mark those items you are willing to work on with an asterisk. Consider a new hairstyle, a touch of hair dye, a tattoo, cosmetic surgery, dieting, a fitness regime, hypnotherapy to lose weight or quit smoking, contact lenses etc, all of which can make a huge difference to your self-esteem.

158 Stop talking about things you dislike about your appearance. Moaning about something is not the same as doing something about it! If you're not willing to *do* something, shut up. No one else wants to hear about it!

159 Take a good look at the way you dress. Do you wear what a confident person would? Try a new image, a change of style. Wear what would make you feel better. Confident people enjoy looking their best and know it does wonders for their confidence and self-esteem.

160 Reflect on how much you are at ease with your sexuality. Working on your physical self-image is the key to sexual fulfilment. Sexual confidence is not about being comfortable with the other person, but about being comfortable with yourself.

161 It is absolutely essential to *stop making comparisons*. Be aware of the physical capabilities you do have – can you walk, see, hear, speak? Millions can't, so be grateful. You're unique. Why not enhance your uniqueness?

A rusty old car?

At a recent seminar the leader referred to the body as 'the temple of the soul, a sacred dwelling place for the spirit.' A young man seated at the back of the hall raised his hand: 'I've always thought of mine as a vehicle,' he said. 'It carries me through life, then goes rusty and packs up. I certainly don't see it as a temple.' He went on to describe the health problems he had endured for years, which showed no sign of abating.

One of the other participants, an elderly lady who looked in radiant good health, spoke up. 'If you think of your body as a rusty old car,' she said, 'is it any wonder you're always ill?'

24 Get in shape

Getting in shape physically is a wonderful way of building your confidence and self-image. It's not easy to feel confident if you're overweight, and exhausted after climbing a flight of stairs.

Health and fitness are just like any other areas of life: get the *causes* right and the *effects* come right too. This means, for instance, sensible eating, good breathing and posture, regular exercise and plenty of laughter and relaxation.

The recipe for better health, maximum energy, minimum illness and an extended lifespan has a familiar ring to it:

- Choose fitness: make it your **intention** to be healthy.
- **Think** health and fitness.
- **Imagine** yourself in peak condition.
- **Act 'as if'** you want to be as fit and healthy as possible.

Give your body what it needs, and it will return the favour!

A vigorous walk will do more for an unhappy but otherwise healthy adult than all the medicine and psychology in the world.

Paul Dudley White

---

162 Consider:

- How healthy are you?
- Have you always been this way? If not, what's changed?
- How important to you is your health?
- What are you willing to do to improve it?

Make a firm commitment to do whatever is necessary to improve your health and fitness levels.

---

163 Think 'health'. Drop all thoughts of illness and disease, and use these affirmations, or make up your own:

'I love my body. I take good care of it. I feel better every day.'
'My body is strong and healthy. Health and wellbeing fill every cell of my body.'

---

164 Relax and imagine your body totally healthy, bursting with energy, no pain or discomfort, enabling you to live a full and active life. Spend a few moments every day creating a mental image of yourself at optimum health and fitness. Once this image permeates the subconscious, it sends healing energy to every cell of your body.

165

A poor diet lowers the body's resistance to disease, drains it of energy and inhibits the efficient workings of the brain. Educate your taste buds to appreciate fresh, nutritious, easily digested, cruelty-free foods and keep the poisons (chemical additives, artificial sweeteners, etc) out of your system.

The ideal diet for most people is approximately 60% fresh fruit and vegetables, 20-25% whole grains, 10% (maximum) protein foods and 10% (maximum) fats. Compare these proportions with your current eating habits. What changes do you need to make?

166

Drink small amounts frequently. The equivalent of eight average sized glasses of water a day boosts the metabolic rate (burning more calories), eliminates waste cells from the body, improves skin tone and deters a host of minor ailments. Go easy on the alcohol. Avoid drinking at mealtimes (this dilutes the digestive juices), especially tea and coffee which inhibit mineral absorption.

167

A plentiful supply of fresh, clean air is essential for good health. Deep breathing supplies much-needed oxygen to the brain and helps eliminate waste products and dead cells.

Do some deep breathing every day. Fill your lungs completely, expanding your ribs and stomach outward, and hold for a count of four. Breathe out through the mouth. Gradually increase the count from four to six, eight, or ten (if comfortable). Do ten of these deep breaths at least three times every day. (NB: if you start feeling dizzy or faint, stop at once.)

168

Get fit. You gain a terrific feeling of confidence and wellbeing from knowing you look good and can cope physically with life's demands.

Take regular exercise. It builds stamina and fitness, increases your resistance to disease and promotes a more youthful appearance. It releases endorphins (the 'happy hormones') into the bloodstream, bringing a feeling of general wellbeing. Commit yourself to taking at least 20 minutes' aerobic exercise every day. Choose something you enjoy – walking, cycling, swimming, dancing or whatever.

Just 20 minutes aerobic exercise a day is quite sufficient to enable most people to maintain good health

Make small adjustments to your lifestyle. Leave the car at home. Walk or cycle to work. Get off the bus a few stops earlier. Replace the electric lawn mower with a manual. Use the stairs instead of the lift. It's not hard to find convenient ways of being more active.

Spend a few moments daily bending and stretching to loosen the muscles and keep them supple. Buy an exercise video or audio tape, for example, of simple yoga exercises which are extremely beneficial and are not that time-consuming.

Once you've started, don't stop. It's easier to get out of shape than into it. It only takes a couple of weeks of inactivity to fall back to where you started.

25 Calmness and confidence

Calmness and confidence are very closely related, and they start with *physical* relaxation. When your body is relaxed, your mind is calmer and clearer, you are more in control of your emotions and better able to relate to others. Physical relaxation and mental calmness help you cope with stressful situations, release unrealistic fears and anxieties, and improve concentration and creativity.

To acquire these benefits for yourself, you must practise:

1. *Entering a peaceful, deeply relaxed state* so that you can recharge your batteries. Make the most of techniques such as **autosuggestion, mental rehearsal, anchoring** and **reframing** (see index).

2. *Instant calmers*. Learn to calm down instantly and stay calm, so that you can deal with awkward people and situations with ease.

Fortunately these skills are easily learned. Most of the early problems you may encounter will disappear if you practise daily, and you will soon be able to relax quickly and easily whenever you have the need.

And remember – the world won't fall apart if you take it easy for a while!

If you are committed to your personal growth, you must have some quiet time to yourself every day. Make it a priority.

David Lawrence Preston

169 Practise this simple method of relaxation every day *without fail* until it comes naturally. It's called *The Five Deep Breaths Technique*.

Take yourself to a quiet place where you will be undisturbed. Have a good stretch, then sit or lie down comfortably. Take a few deep breaths. Focus your gaze on a spot on the ceiling. When your eyes start to tire, let them close.

Now take a very deep breath. Say 'one' and let it out slowly, relaxing the eye muscles, face and neck. Pause for a moment, then take an even deeper breath. Say 'two' and let it out slowly, relaxing your shoulders, arms and hands. Pause and take a third deep breath. Say 'three' and let it out slowly, relaxing all the muscles in your legs and feet. Now take a fourth deep breath. Say 'four' and let it out slowly, relaxing all the muscles in your entire body.

Now take a fifth deep breath. Say 'five' and let it out slowly, whispering the word 'relax' under your breath. If you feel a little light-headed, or your arms and legs feel slightly heavy, good! Now, while you continue to go deeper into relaxation imagine you are in a quiet, peaceful place, such as a beach or garden, or in a special sanctuary or cosy country cottage. Put your thumb and fingers together and slowly whisper the following words several times:

'One. Two. Three. Relax. Relax.'

If you practise every day, within a week or two you'll be able to relax deeply whenever you wish. All you'll have to do is close your eyes, take a deep breath, put your thumb and fingers together and quietly say, 'One. Two. Three. Relax. Relax.'

170 This method is called ***Differential Relaxation***. Make yourself comfortable, take a deep breath and close your eyes. Each time you breathe in, tense a group of muscles as hard as you can for five seconds. As you exhale, say the word 'relax' or 'calm' under your breath and feel the tension flowing out, leaving the muscles heavy and relaxed. Notice the difference between tension and relaxation.

- Tense and relax the feet, curling your toes under as tightly as you can.

- Tense and relax the lower legs.

- Tense and relax the upper legs.

- Tighten and relax the hips and buttocks.

- Tighten and relax your stomach muscles.

- Arch your back and tighten and relax the muscles.

- Tense and relax the hands, clenching your fists tightly.

- Tense and relax the forearms, pushing outward as if pressing against an invisible wall.

- Tense and relax the upper arms.

- Bend your elbows and tense and relax your biceps.

- Shrug your shoulders up to your ears and relax them.

- Tense and relax the neck.

- Tense and relax the face, closing your eyes as tightly as you can, wrinkling the forehead and drawing the corners of your mouth back.

Now imagine your body as a rag doll, limp and floppy, your muscles soft and loose, no tension. Slowly count down from ten to one on each out breath. You may also find it helpful to imagine some simple scene, somewhere full of peace and tranquillity, such as a place in the country, a garden, beach or special sanctuary.

171

When you are deeply relaxed repeat the following suggestions slowly to yourself.

'I relax easily, quickly and deeply. Each time I relax, I go deeper and deeper. My thinking is peaceful, calm and centred.'

This conditions your subconscious and helps you relax easily.

172

After each session, reflect on the relaxation.

- How did you feel before you started?
- What did you think about during the session?
- Was your mind totally still at any point?
- How do you feel now?

173

Breathing is the key to instant calmness and relaxation. Attention to your breath helps you to become aware of your body, focuses your concentration and brings your mind back to the present.

Take three very slow, deep breaths. Breathe out slowly, saying the word 'relax' under your breath, until your lungs are empty. Breathe normally for a few breaths. Then repeat the three slow breaths. Return to your activities feeling relaxed and calm.

174

Practise this. Take a deep breath and let it out slowly. Then repeat this affirmation:

'I am cool, calm, confident and in control.'

The more you practise, the more effective it will be when you need it.

175

Write down this sentence:

'As I become a calmer and more relaxed person, I am becoming aware...'

Quickly write down the first six thoughts that come into your head.

26 | Anchoring

Anchoring is a way of drawing on past experiences in which you felt confident to help you cope better in the present. It's another powerful weapon in your confidence armoury.

An anchor is any stimulus that consistently triggers an emotion. To use an anchor you have to:

- Generate in yourself the particular *set of feelings* you wish to recreate.

- *Programme your subconscious* to associate those feelings with specific words and gestures.

- Use those words and gestures to *trigger the desired feelings* when required.

Sportsmen and women use anchors continually. For example, tennis players bounce the ball repeatedly before serving to calm themselves; most runners go through an elaborate routine to centre themselves, much of which is not strictly necessary to the actual performance; and the mighty All Black rugby team go through a series of rituals before each match to intimidate the opposition and fire themselves up.

You constantly anchor feelings in the nervous system whether you like it or not, so why not learn to use this to your advantage? Using anchors you can feel *calm* and confident, or *energised* and confident whenever you wish.

People tell me I'm lucky, but I've noticed
the harder I practise, the luckier I get.

Gary Player

176 When you brought your thumb and fingers together and whispered One. Two. Three. Relax. Relax.' (Confidence Builder No. 169) you were, in fact, installing an anchor.

Practise this every day until you are able to calm yourself down simply by taking a deep breath, placing your thumb and fingers together, breathing out slowly and saying 'One. Two. Three. Relax. Relax.' This will take a couple of weeks to perfect, but it's well worth it. It's a priceless skill.

177 Install an anchor which energises you.

Relax your body, and either recall or imagine a situation in which you felt 100% charged and at your best. Bring to mind all the associated sights, sounds, smells and physical sensations as vividly as possible.

Then 'anchor' those feelings. Choose a gesture you wouldn't normally use (not the thumb and fingers, your subconscious associates this with calm). I use a clenched fist. Make the gesture and whisper a phrase such as 'Yes! Yes! Yes!'

178 Keep practising and, within a few weeks, whenever you clench your fist and say, 'Yes! Yes! Yes!' you'll feel a surge of energy, physical and emotional.

179 Choose an event you shortly have to face, when you need to remain calm, but you fear could bring on nervousness.

Start working on your anchor a few weeks before the event. Get into the relaxed state and recall a time when you felt really calm and confident. Relive it in as much detail as possible. If you can't think of a suitable time just *pretend* to be confident. If you have a good imagination, your subconscious won't know the difference.

When the feeling is strong, put your thumb and fingers together and gently whisper, 'Cool, calm and confident'. The stronger the feeling, the more successful will be your anchor. Affirm that *every time you make this gesture and repeat these words, these same calm, confident feelings will return.*

This is called 'installing the anchor'.

180 Practise anchoring every day until it comes easily to you. The more practice, the better.

181 Just before the actual event you were rehearsing in Confidence Builder 179, and if necessary during it, take a deep breath, put your thumb and fingers together and repeat your chosen phrase silently or aloud. Say it *with conviction.* Allow the confident feelings to flow through you. This is called 'firing' the anchor.

182 Alternatively, install an anchor when you experience good feelings as you go about your activities. This is effectively what athletes do when they raise their hands above their heads as they break the winning tape. If they were to do this repeatedly they would find that simply raising their hands above their heads would trigger those winning feelings.

'Making up for lost time'

Six years ago, Angela Dennett felt like a prisoner in her own home. Despite a debilitating back condition she was on full-time duty caring for her husband, who suffered from Altzheimer's disease. When he died, she found herself with time on her hands, looking for something to get her out of the house.

As a young woman she would have liked a career in academia. She had a passionate interest in Ancient Egypt, but lacked confidence and grew up thinking it was beyond her. She ended up in a mind numbing office job.

One day Angela picked up a leaflet about the University of the Third Age (U3A), which provided educational and social activities for the over 50s. One of the courses was Creating Confidence. With trepidation she enrolled and diligently applied what she learned. Soon after the Membership Secretary's job became vacant, and she put herself forward. A few months later, she was elected Chairman. 'At first I was terrified,' she said. 'It takes a lot of confidence to control committee meetings, but I soon learned.'

It was then that her interest in Egyptology came to the fore. 'After my husband died, I was able to study it properly. I enrolled for a degree course with the Open University, then I took the plunge and started teaching – I wouldn't have had the confidence before. I gained a teaching certificate and am now a qualified adult education tutor.'

She regularly went to London to attend talks by the leading authorities. 'One day I thought, why should I have to travel all this way, so I started the Wessex Ancient Egypt Society. Now the experts come to us.'

Recently a dream came true when Angela was invited to visit Egypt. 'I'd never flown before because I was too scared, but I wasn't going to let that stop me, I used the techniques I'd learned on the confidence course – positive thinking, relaxation, visualisation and small steps to conquer my phobia. I was fine.'

'As I see it, I'm in the second half of my life now, and fast trying to make up for lost time.' And how!

27 So far, so good

We're just over half way now. What have you learned about confidence? More importantly, what have you learned about yourself? If you've understood what you've read so far *and put it into practice*, your confidence and self-esteem have already grown.

Take a pen and paper, and give yourself a mark out of ten, where ten means you feel you could achieve anything and zero that you feel useless at everything.

Now give yourself another mark out of ten, where ten means you feel worthy of good things and zero completely undeserving.

Now give yourself a mark out of ten for how well you relate to others.

Compare these marks with what you gave yourself six months ago (Confidence Builders 8, 9 and 10). See what I mean about your confidence and self-esteem having grown?

After pausing to take stock we'll take a more in-depth look at the ITIA Formula©, introduce additional insights and techniques, then discuss skills that will help you to communicate confidently. Soon you'll be ready to take on the world and pursue whatever your heart desires.

By accepting yourself and joyfully being what you are, you fulfil your own abilities, and your simple presence can make others happy.

Jane Roberts

183 In Section 3 you made one of the most important decisions of your life: to work on your confidence and self-esteem. Reaffirm your promise to yourself to:

- Always treat yourself with love and respect.

- Act as if you could achieve anything you put your mind to.

- Accept only the best for yourself.

184 Make a list of all the good things that have happened to you since you started reading this book. How many of them are due to your increased confidence?

185 List six ways in which your confidence has risen. What more needs to change? What are you doing to change them? What more do you need to do?

186 List six ways in which you are taking better care of yourself than you were six months ago, and six ways in which you could take even better care of yourself. Now put them into practice.

187

Look out for self-help groups, talks and courses on confidence in your area (eg adult education courses, university extra-mural departments, assertiveness training etc). Enrol for one of these at the next available opportunity.

If there's nothing suitable locally, write to me for details of the audiotape based home study course, the DLP Audio Programme.

188

How are you getting on with the tools and techniques you have learned?

- How much time do you allocate to building your confidence each day. How can you increase it? The more time and effort you invest, the more rapid your progress.

- How are you getting on with the ITIA Formula© and the Four Step Method? What benefits have you gained so far?

- What improvements have you made using affirmations?

- What affirmations are you currently using?

- How do you feel now about the incidents you reframed?

- How quickly and deeply do you relax when you use the Five Deep Breaths or Differential Relaxation techniques? Keep practising.

- How quickly can you calm yourself when you need to? Keep practising.

- How well do the triggers, 'One. Two. Three. Relax. Relax.' and 'Cool, calm and confident.' work for you?

- How effective is the clenched fist energiser 'Yes! Yes! Yes!'?

- What other anchors have you installed for yourself?

- What more do you need to do?

189

You've also gained many practical confidence-building suggestions:

- In Confidence Builder 21, I asked you to choose something that makes you nervous and do it. What did you choose? Did you actually do it? What happened? (If you didn't, do it now!)

- Look at your list of goals (Confidence Builders 31 and 93). What have you done about them? How far have you come? What more do you need to do?

- Give three examples of how you've used mental rehearsal to help you cope with difficult situations. What were the outcomes? What further use could you make of the technique? How could you do it better next time?

- Whom did you choose to model? How is it going? What have you gained?

- In Confidence Builder 91, you decided to become an expert in something. What did you choose? How much time and thought have you given it? What progress have you made? Keep working on it.

- How are you getting on with your chosen hobbies (Example 133)?

- How's your physical self-image improvement programme going? Are you sticking at it? What more do you need to do?

28 Find a purpose

How would you feel if everything you were ever going to be, you are right now? If everything you are going to achieve, you have already achieved? Life would be pretty meaningless, wouldn't it?

There's nothing more important than finding a purpose that inspires and motivates you and gives your life meaning and direction. There's nothing more soul destroying than drifting through life with nothing to strive for, no ambitions, no goals. Aimlessness destroys confidence and self-esteem.

When you find what you love to do and put your heart and soul into it, everything changes. Life becomes fulfilling and exciting. If your purpose benefits others as well as yourself, everything, yes, *everything* falls perfectly into place. If your motives are sound, happiness and prosperity simply flow towards you; nothing can stop them.

If you're not aware of having a purpose, it's not because you don't have one; everyone has. It's because you've never looked for it. *It's lying dormant somewhere in your consciousness, waiting to be revealed.*

We act as though comfort and luxury are the chief requirements of life, when all that we need to make us really happy is something to be enthusiastic about.

Charles Kingsley

190 Do you have an overall sense of purpose that benefits others as well as yourself? Something you love doing and can put your heart and soul into? If so, write it down on a small card and keep it with you.

191 Think about your values. Clarifying your values is the starting point of finding your purpose. Values are simply what you believe to be important.

What is most important to you in life? What do you stand for? Where do your priorities lie? How important are, say, your health or family relationships compared with your career, or your social and leisure activities compared with your spiritual life?

192 If you're not sure of the answers to Confidence Builder 191, go inside and get in touch with your intuition, the part that *knows*. Relax your body, calm your mind and ask, 'What is most important to me in life? Where do my priorities lie? What is my purpose for being here?'

Remain quiet for five or ten minutes. Listen patiently and attentively to your inner self. Answers may not come immediately, but they will if you're patient.

193 Which, if any, of your values are you having difficulty living up to at present? In what way(s)? What would you like to change?

194 Write down the answers to these questions:

- What talents and skills do I have? How can I make better use of them?

- If I could change anything at all that would benefit others as well as myself, what would it be?

- Suppose I had only three more months to live. How would I most like to spend my remaining time?

Write yourself a letter explaining why you are not already doing these things.

195 Write down your 'life mission statement' in no more than three sentences.

Think laterally. For instance, if you're a hairdresser your mission is more than cutting hair: it's to make people feel good about themselves; if a decorator or gardener, to create a more attractive environment; if a teacher, to help raise the self-esteem of young people and give them the best chance of a happy life.

Write your mission on a small card, pin it to your Wall of Confidence and read it every day.

(Here's mine as an example: 'My mission is to spread peace, love and happiness, to encourage people to live life to the full and help others to do the same. I do this through my writing, teaching, tape programmes, therapy and all my personal contacts.')

196 Minimise your contacts with people who have no sense of purpose and vision of their own. They will drag you down and damage your self-esteem if you let them.

Cherish the freedom to be yourself. Be guided by your inner voice and do what you believe in. Sing, dance and embrace life to the full.

Linda Kelham

Be a first-rate you, not a second-rate someone else!

George Gershwin, the famous jazz pianist, composer and songwriter, had ambitions as a classical musician, so he approached Maurice Ravel, composer of the famous Bolero, for instruction in orchestral scoring. After several lessons, Ravel was exasperated. His student appeared unable to grasp even the basics.

'If I were you,' he advised his student, 'I would be happier to be a first rate Gershwin than a second rate Ravel'.

29 Goals revisited

Practical goals build confidence and put you more in control of your life. When you set yourself a goal, even if you've never thought about it before, you unleash powerful mental forces. You accomplish more, often much more. Even if all you did was write down a goal and file the piece of paper away in a drawer, your life would be different in some way.

Why do ***clear, realistic goals*** make such a difference?

1. They clarify your purpose.

2. They show you're serious about achieving.

3. They stimulate excitement, anticipation, energy and enthusiasm.

4. They help to keep your mind on what you want. Goals impress your desires on the subconscious, heighten your awareness and highlight opportunities you may previously have missed.

5. They prompt you to acquire new knowledge and skills.

6. You discover reservoirs of imagination and creativity you previously didn't realise you had.

You first came across goal setting in Section 5. Now you're going to take it further.

I believe you came into the world to accomplish
something, and not something small or insignificant.
That's not worthy of you. You came here to make
a major contribution to life on this planet.

Paul Solomon

197 Take a fresh look at the goals you listed in your notebook. Are they still relevant? Anything to add? What else would you like to achieve?

Modify your list if appropriate. Write them down. PRINT THEM IN CAPITALS (check back to Exercise 67 to remind yourself of the reason for this). Use clear language, avoiding nebulous words and phrases such as 'I want to help people'. Exactly how do you want to help them?

198 Aim high, but bear in mind that many people with low self-esteem make unrealistic demands on themselves. They become frustrated by the gap between their aspirations and their actual accomplishments.

For example, you may be concerned about homeless people, but you can't house them all personally, nor raise enough money to solve the problem on your own. Concentrate on what you can do, and don't assume that if you can't save the whole of humankind, you've failed.

199 Take each goal (Confidence Builder 197) in turn and list all the benefits that achieving it will bring you, your family and the wider community. Remember, the more benefits you can identify, the greater the pulling power of your goal.

200 Work backwards from each goal in Confidence Builder 197, break it down into small steps, and establish a time scale for the completion of each step.

201 Keep your goals to yourself, unless you think another person can offer practical help and encouragement. There is only one exception: if your goal is to rid yourself of a bad habit, such as smoking, swearing or losing your temper, tell everyone. People won't be slow to remind you if you slip up!

202 Do something every day towards your goals, and don't forget to spend a few minutes each day visualising yourself succeeding. This is particularly effective last thing at night, because it gives the subconscious something to work on while you are sleep.

203 Don't let your self-worth depend on your achievements. People with high self-esteem don't feel they have to prove themselves by high attainment. They feel good about themselves even if they don't succeed at everything.

There's nothing wrong with *wanting* to achieve, but people who are driven by a *need* to achieve rarely find true happiness even when they do succeed. Have a go, but don't become obsessive. Do it because you enjoy it, learn from it and grow.

The greatest pleasure in life is doing what people say you cannot do.

Walter Bagehot

Shoot for the moon!

When President Kennedy challenged America to put a man on the Moon within a decade and return him safely to Earth, learned eyebrows were raised because the technology needed did not exist at the time. However, the decision to set a firm goal spurred the scientific community into action. Inspired by their President's vision, scientists who had considered it impossible changed their mentality from, 'It can't be done' to 'How can we make this happen?'

Similarly, when you set yourself a goal it is not necessary to have all the know-how and resources at your disposal. All that is required is enthusiasm and persistence, then the essential ingredients somehow show up to make it possible. And just as the new technologies developed for the Moon shot affected other areas of our lives, working towards a worthwhile goal has many unforeseen benefits, not least an enormous growth in confidence.

30 The Thinker thinks and the Prover proves

Most thoughts come from the subconscious, that hive of mental activity that lies below the threshold of momentary awareness. You cannot prevent a thought floating up from the subconscious; this is beyond your conscious control.

However, **you can always choose whether to accept, reject or ignore a thought**, whether to voice it or act on it. Any pattern of thought or action which is repeated often is impressed on the subconscious and becomes a habit. Likewise, when you withdraw your attention from an unwanted thought or habit, it eventually withers and dies.

You constantly refer to your subconscious store of thoughts and memories for information and guidance, which sets up a cycle in which what you repeatedly think about tends to intensify in your experience.

The conscious mind is the **Thinker**; the subconscious is the **Prover**. If, for example, you hold the thought 'I'm not very clever', the subconscious looks for evidence that you are what you think you are. Consequently you steer clear of anything that requires intelligence, which 'proves' you were right all along. Except, of course, *you may be misleading yourself.* You may actually be far cleverer than you think you are!

That's why it's so important to turn your thinking around, by deliberately and consciously planting confident thoughts in your mind. When you let go of disempowering, confidence-draining thoughts and start thinking of yourself as strong, capable, likable and deserving, the cycle is reversed.

Argue for your limitations, and they're yours.

Richard Carlson

204 Think back over your life. How often have you *thought* something was beyond your capabilities, so you backed off, only to realise later that you could have succeeded if you'd tried? Can you recall what you told yourself at the time?

205 Silence the Inner Critic with encouraging, supportive but *realistic* self-talk. For instance:

- Change 'I can't' to 'I can'. If this is too big a leap, try:
- 'Perhaps 1 would find it difficult at present, but I can learn.'
- 'There must be a way. Let's look at the alternatives.'
- 'I can't (eg play the violin), but only because I've never tried. I'm sure I could learn.'
- 'Please show me how. I'm willing to learn.'

This way you give the Prover something positive to work with and open up a new world of possibilities.

206 If you make a mistake, and everyone does, don't chastise yourself. Instead, learn from it and look for a better way for the future.

207 Listen carefully to your self-talk and become aware of censorious questions such as:

- 'What did I do (or say) that for, idiot?'

- 'What's the use?'

- 'Why am I so stupid?'

- 'Why does this always happen to me?'

- 'Why does everyone hate me?'

Questions such as these are based on the supposition that you are an idiot, or you have screwed up (again). The Prover is not programmed to challenge the basis of a question; it responds as if it were true. For example, if you ask yourself 'Why am I so stupid?' the Prover finds a multitude of reasons why you are stupid even though you're not. That's what it's designed to do.

Instead, cancel the question using Thought Stopping, and give your subconscious something positive to work on, eg:

- 'What can I learn from this?'

- 'What can I do *now* to feel more confident?'

- 'How would a confident person handle this situation?'

- 'How can I improve?'

When problems arise, focus your mind on finding solutions by asking yourself the right questions:

- 'What can I do to solve this problem?'

- 'How can I turn it to my advantage?'

- 'What more do I need to know?'

These compel the Prover to work *for* rather than against you.

208 Stop apologising for yourself. Don't let phrases such as the following ever pass your lips:

- 'It's *only* me!' Don't diminish yourself in this way. Just say 'it's me!'
- 'I'm sorry to trouble you, but...'
- 'I'm afraid...'
- 'I know it's not very good, but...'
- 'I don't want to be any trouble, but...'

209 Don't apologise for what you do well. Avoid boasting, of course, but don't knock your achievements or devalue your experiences. The Prover takes these as instructions to ease off, and could unintentionally sabotage your efforts.

Be justly proud of your achievements, then the Prover assumes you want more of the same.

210 Stop thinking of yourself as a victim. If you're determined to be one, you always be. If you ever feel like a victim, use this affirmation:

'I was *not* brought into the world to be a victim, and I am *not* a victim.'

Write it in your notebook, and pin it to your Wall of Confidence.

Henry Ford famously remarked

'Whether you think you can, or you think you can't, you're quite right.'

31 Confident self-talk

When you think like a confident person, you automatically feel more confident and act more confidently. Makes sense, doesn't it?

Confident self-talk includes any language that helps you feel better and cope more easily. Words and sentences that imply that you are helpless or incapable, or that things are worse than they actually are, feed the Prover with potentially damaging ammunition, which is why the negative thought patterns discussed in this section come with a health warning.

The following thoughts destroy confidence and damage self-esteem.

Simple linguistic changes such as those described in this section are often derided as superficial, but can make a huge difference to the way you handle yourself. And remember: you're not trying to pull the wool over your eyes, just adopt a more constructive, confident point of view.

*If you keep on saying things are going to be bad,
you have a good chance of being a prophet.*

Isaac Bashevis Singer

211

Among the most pernicious phrases to be aware of are those containing 'should', 'shouldn't' and their close relatives, 'ought', 'must', 'got to', 'have to', 'mustn't,' 'supposed to,' etc and their negations 'oughtn't', 'mustn't' and so on.

If you live your life by 'shoulds' and 'shouldn'ts', you're probably not living in the real world. You have to deal with things as they are, not how you think they should be.

There are two types of 'should'. The first refers to you, your achievements and your conduct. For instance:

- 'I *should* be different from how I am.'

- 'I *should* be better than I am.'

- 'I *mustn't....*'

- 'To be happy I *must....*'

These infer that fixed rules limit your options, or that someone else is making your choices for you. Change them to 'I want to…', 'I don't want to…', 'I choose/choose not to…', or 'I prefer/prefer not to…'

212

Make a list of all the things you think you 'should' do, in other words, the rules by which you choose to live. Take each in turn and ask yourself, 'Why should I?'
Now rewrite your list:

- Replacing 'should' with 'could'.

- Using the phrase, 'If I really wanted to, I could…'

How do you feel about the items on your list now?

213 Other 'shoulds' relate to life, other people and the world in general:

- 'She *should* have done better.'
- 'He *shouldn't* behave like that.'
- 'Things *should* be different.'
- 'Someone *should* do something about it!'

These invariably lead to disappointment, since it is unrealistic to expect the world to conform to your wishes, and you'll never feel good about yourself if you constantly disapprove of everyone and wish everything were different.

214 If you're a 'should' sort of person it probably means you were raised by dominant parents and haven't yet broken free.

Every time you become aware of a should or shouldn't thought, silent or voiced, stop. Ask yourself, 'Where did that thought come from? Where's the evidence that this is how it *should* be?' You'll usually find there isn't any!

215 Stop generalising. eg

- 'I always...'
- 'You never...'
- 'You always...'
- 'They never...'

Keep things in proportion. Just because you've made one mistake doesn't mean you never get anything right, and if someone treats you badly it doesn't mean everyone hates you. Don't assume just because one person has been unfair that the whole world is against you.

216 Avoid black and white thinking. For example, you may not succeed 100% of the time, but this doesn't mean you never achieve anything worthwhile. You can learn from everything you do; everything has some value for you.

217 Stop exaggerating and over-dramatising. Veto phrases such as:

- 'It's awful, terrible, hopeless.'
- 'It's a catastrophe, complete disaster, total fiasco.'
- 'I've blown it!'

Replace with kinder, gentler, more optimistic forms of words:

- 'It's a little unfortunate.'
- 'I'm a bit disappointed.'
- 'It's not what I would have wanted, but it's OK.'
- 'I've had a slight setback/a few minor problems to overcome.'
- 'There must be a way. What are the alternatives?'

32 Beliefs

A *belief* is a collection of thoughts that we accept as true. Most of our beliefs have their origins in childhood conditioning and our cultural background: they were absorbed without any effort on our part. Others were acquired as we matured and learned to interpret the world for ourselves.

Your beliefs affect everything you do:

- Confident people believe they can be whatever they want to be and accomplish anything they choose. Even if their goals seem far off, they believe that everything is eventually attainable.

- Believing you cannot do something makes you incapable of doing it. But it is not your actual abilities that determine the outcome, but what you *believe* about them.

- Negative beliefs are like the automatic brakes fitted to certain vehicles. Just as you're about to break through old barriers, on come the brakes!

It's vital to *let go of beliefs which destroy your confidence*, and it's perfectly possible. Fortunately, no belief is permanently engraved on your brain. All beliefs are learned, and all learning can be re-evaluated and updated.

As soon as you adopt a new belief the Prover sets to work to validate the new belief. Suddenly all the incoming evidence supports your new way of thinking, and anything which contradicts it is rejected or ignored.

Men often become what they believe themselves to be. If I believe I cannot do something, it makes me incapable of doing it. When I believe I can, I acquire the ability to do it even if I didn't have it in the beginning.

Mahatma Gandhi

218

The most disempowering belief is that lack of confidence comes with your genes and is *just the way you are*. This is a complete misconception, although quite a common one.

This is so important, I must repeat: your genes play a role in deciding whether you are more introverted or extroverted; volatile or placid; and prone to certain conditions such as depression and compulsive behaviours.

But genes do not determine confidence. Confidence (or lack of it) comes from what you believe about yourself. *No causal link has ever been found between genes and confidence.*

219

You can re-condition any belief that interferes with your confidence, happiness and self-esteem using the ITIA Formula©:

- Be clear on the beliefs that need to change, and with what you intend to replace them.

- Dispute the old beliefs and adopt a new way of thinking.

- Imagine yourself acting on the new belief and getting the desired results.

- Act as if you totally accept the new belief. The more your behaviour is consistent with a belief, the more unshakable it becomes.

220 Quickly write down five positive and five negative beliefs you hold about yourself.

221 Which, if any, of the beliefs from Confidence Builder 220 bring unhappiness, reduce your effectiveness, destroy relationships or detract from your quality of life?

Cross out each disempowering belief and write down its opposite. Turn it into an affirmation, commencing with the words 'I believe in myself'. For example:

■ 'I believe in myself. I am attractive.'

■ 'I believe in myself. I am courageous.'

■ 'I believe in myself. I am intelligent.'

222 Practise disputing disempowering beliefs. Disputing a negative belief means examining its validity. It may be based on incorrect or misleading information, so look for different explanations and meanings. Ask yourself:

■ Where's the evidence?

■ Did I miss something?

■ What positive value could it have?

■ What could I learn from it that will benefit me?

■ Does it really matter anyway?

223 Think about your disempowering beliefs and complete these sentences with several endings:

■ 'If this belief were really true...'

■ 'If this belief turned out to be false...'

224 Every day relax and imagine the effect of your updated, positive beliefs on your life. 'See', 'hear' and 'feel' yourself behaving differently as your confidence improves. Whenever you have an opportunity to put your new beliefs into practice, act as if they are definitely true.

It's official – the bumble bee can't fly!

According to the theory of aerodynamics, the bumble bee is totally unable to fly. Laboratory experiments prove this conclusively. The size, weight and shape of the bee's body in relation to the size of its wings makes flying impossible.

Moral: Lack of belief in our abilities and worrying about the outcome are the main impediments to success.

The bumble bee, being ignorant of the theory, flies anyway!

33 Confident attitudes

Attitudes and **beliefs**, while closely related, are not exactly the same. A belief is a thought or mental image we accept as true. An attitude is what you put out into the world through your words and actions.

For example, a belief such as 'I'm not good enough' will manifest in your speech and behaviour. *That's* when it becomes an attitude. In addition, attitudes involve a degree of evaluation, in other words, what you feel about the belief.

A positive attitude shows in everything you do – how you walk, talk, what you say, how you say it, and the way others see you. It builds confidence and success in every area of your life. When you conquer attitudes of doubt and fear you effectively conquer feelings of failure. And the good news is, positive attitudes can be developed, using the Four Step Method and the ITIA Formula©.

This section spells out **seven attitudes** which are essential for confidence, self-esteem, happiness and peace of mind. Learn and apply them.

Nothing is good or bad, but thinking makes it so.

William Shakespeare

---

225 Everything that happens to me – favourable or not – helps me to learn and to grow. It's my attitude towards it that counts. I am grateful for every challenge that comes my way.

I respond to everything that happens with the question 'What can I learn from this?', especially anything that troubles me.

---

226 I love being better – not better than others, but better than I was before. No one is better than anyone else, only different. No one is more deserving of happiness than I.

---

227 I like myself. I'm kind and considerate towards myself. I take good care of myself. I'm proud to be me, and I love who I am. That's how I find peace and contentment from within.

---

228 I believe in myself. I can do anything I choose – if not now, I can learn. I think, speak and act confidently at all times.

---

229 My self-worth does not depend on others' approval or on what others say or do. I am not here to conform to other people's expectations. I nourish myself with love, approval and self-worth.

230 My self-worth does not depend on my achievements, nor do I allow it to be diminished by failure. That's why I'm happy to take risks, feel the fear and have a go anyway.

231 I am accepted, and I respect others. I accept and relate to them as they are and don't try to change them.

Attitude

The longer I live, the more I realise the impact of attitude on life.

Attitude, to me, is more important than facts. It is more important than the past, than education, than money, than circumstances, than failure, than successes, than what other people think or say or do. It is more important than appearance, giftedness or skill.

The remarkable thing is we have a choice every day regarding the attitude we will embrace for that day. We cannot change our past. We cannot change the fact that people will act in a certain way. We cannot change the inevitable. The only thing we can do is play on the one string we have, and that is our attitude.

I am convinced that life is 10% what happens to me and 90% how I react to it. And so it is with you... we are in charge of our attitudes!

Charles Swindoll

I now release easily and effortlessly all my old negative attitudes and beliefs.

34 Self-love

Some people think it's a sin to love yourself. They consider those who love themselves to be selfish, conceited and rather unpleasant. But they're mistaken. They confuse self-love with false pride and narcissism (being in love *with* yourself) which is quite a different matter. Vanity and arrogance are usually a form of bravado engaged in by people who love themselves too little and are trying to cover it up.

If you don't love yourself you'll have no sense of **self-worth**, and no feeling of acceptance or belonging.

Furthermore, your capacity for loving others is directly related to how much love you have for yourself. You can't share anything you don't have. How can you truly love another if you don't feel worthy of giving and receiving love? Impossible.

The belief that you need to be different from how you are in order to be loved causes a great deal of misery. Unless you are happy within, you'll never be truly satisfied with what you do. Loving yourself *unconditionally* is the key to happiness. But you don't have to be perfect: the most loved person in the world makes mistakes! You don't even have to do your best. You don't have to prove anything. You're all right because you're all right, and lovable exactly as you are.

It's a funny thing about life:
if you refuse to accept anything less than the best,
you very often get it.

W. Somerset Maugham

232 Reflect on your attitude to loving yourself. Is it OK to love yourself? Or do you consider it sinful? Arrogant? Conceited? If so, from where does this attitude come?

233 Write down this sentence:

'If only I were... then I'd be lovable.'

Quickly, without thinking about it too hard, fill in the gap with whatever comes to mind.
Examine what you've written. Does it really make sense?

234 Think of someone or several people you know who are loud, boastful, arrogant and vain. In your opinion do these people truly love themselves? Or are they *in love with* themselves? Is their outward display nothing more than a cover up?

235 Regularly pamper yourself. Treat yourself to an occasional massage, aromatherapy, sauna, a long soak in the bath, reflexology, a manicure, whatever you fancy. Not only does it help recharge your batteries, but it also reminds you that you deserve the very best.

236

Relax your body. Calm your mind. Imagine there is someone there with you, who loves you, really loves you. This could be a living or deceased person, a spiritual being whom you admire, such as Jesus, Buddha or Mohammed, or a guardian angel. Welcome them. 'Feel' their presence.

Now imagine that this person is telling you how much he or she loves you and all the good things they see in you. Listen carefully. How do you feel?

When you return to full alertness, describe the experience in your notebook.

237

Use these affirmations:

'I am worthy of all the good in my life.'
'I am open and accepting of myself and others.'
'I am loving, lovable and loved.'
'I feel warm and loving towards myself at all times.'

238

Practise TFM – Time For Me. Make time for yourself every day, for relaxing, doing as you please, having fun. This sends a powerful message to the subconscious that you deserve it and you're worth it. Besides, if you don't make time for yourself, who else is going to make time for you?

One of life's losers

Dawn was an attractive woman in her mid-30s, depressed and on the verge of a nervous breakdown. She was well qualified but out of work, had no friends and hardly ever went out. She was also desperate to evict her abusive ex-boyfriend, Nick, from her flat but he was refusing to leave. She described herself as 'one of life's losers'. 'I hate myself,' she said, 'I'm such a failure.'

Naturally I taught her to use the ITIA Formula© and Four Step Method. We also talked about loving yourself. I suggested she used the affirmations suggested in Confidence Builder 237 every day.

Here's what she told me in a letter six months after she quit therapy. 'I now have a job. It's not exactly what I want, but it is well paid and could lead to something more suitable. It's made me feel a lot better. Nick has moved out, and although I'm still seeking an intelligent, good-looking and caring man, I now know that I'm not prepared to settle for any old rubbish like before. I've joined a health club and made new friends, and I go out several times a week with my new flat mate (female) which must be increasing my chances of meeting someone nice. I'm even beginning to love myself.'

When you learn to love yourself change always takes place. Not *always* immediately – but it will.

35 Concentrate on what you do well

To enjoy a better life you must focus on your ***potential***, not your limitations, and concentrate on ***what you do well***. You must make the most of your natural aptitudes and abilities.

Of course everyone has weaknesses, and it takes courage to admit to them. But it can be equally harrowing to accept that we have our strengths and acknowledge that we have talents and personal qualities that others don't have.

This section is about your ***strengths*** and making better use of them. You'll discover you have many on which to build.

The world is full of unsuccessful people who have talent but lack confidence and tenacity, who feel that no matter how good they are at something, someone else is bound to be better. *Don't be one of them.*

It is all too obvious that in the great majority of human beings, the greater part of their possibilities, whether physical or spiritual, intellectual or aesthetic, remains unrealised.

Sir Julian Huxley

239 Head a page of your notebook 'My strengths'. Now write down all your good points, everything you like about yourself. For example, are you a good communicator? A good cook? A talented artist or musician? Good with numbers? Handy with tools or good at fixing things? A sympathetic listener?

Don't hold back. Keep writing until you've thought of *at least two dozen*. Add to your list over the next few days whenever you think of a new strength.

240 Write down this sentence:

'I like myself most when...'

Quickly, without thinking about it too hard, write down the first thoughts that come into your head and add them to your list of strengths.

241 List your strengths as your partner or best friend would see them.

242 Go through your list of strengths (confidence Builder 239), and for each consider:

- How can I make good/better use of this?
- How can I do or use more of this?
- How can I do/use it more often?

Write your answers in your notebook. Think about them. You may wish to amend your goals in the light of these new insights.

243 Make a list of personal qualities you wish to develop or acquire. Take each in turn and work on it for a week using the ITIA Formula©. Begin by making up affirmations that encapsulate the kind of person you wish to become. For example, 'Every day in every way I become more and more *patient*.' Use your affirmations every day.

244 Each day for one week relax and visualise or imagine what it would feel like to have that quality. For instance, imagine how you would feel and behave if you were more patient and how your life would be different.

245 For one week concentrate on behaving as if you already had this new quality or habit. Taking patience as an example, in week one make a determined effort to be more patient. If you slip up, don't worry, just keep trying. Every success, however small, raises your confidence another notch.

In week two go on to the next quality, work on that for a week, and so on. When you reach the bottom of your list, review your progress. Cross off any qualities you feel you've mastered. If you wish, substitute a new one. Then work through your list again.

Keep going, working down your list until you've acquired all the qualities or habits you desire.

The Benjamin Franklin Approach

Shakespeare, who was no mean psychologist, wrote, 'Assume a virtue if you have it not.' This is exactly what Benjamin Franklin, one of the signatories of the American Declaration of Independence, decided to do.

He made a list of 17 personal qualities and habits he wanted to acquire. He realised that it would be too much to attempt all 17 at once, so he worked on one a week. He spent a week practising each new habit, then moved on to the next and worked on that for a week.

When he felt he'd mastered a new habit he dropped it from the list and substituted a new one. After 17 weeks he went back to the top of his list, so by the end of the year he'd completed the entire cycle three times.

Benjamin Franklin had applied:

The As If Principle.

36 Overcoming weaknesses

In Section 22 you made a list of personal 'weaknesses'. Note that I've put the word in inverted commas, since some may not be weaknesses at all, just your perceptions.

Weaknesses come in three types:

- *Important traits which can be worked on*, perhaps even eliminated if you want to and are willing to put in a little time and effort. These include those which originate in conscious attitudes or beliefs, are the result of flawed conditioning, or are basically down to lack of resolve, such as lack of patience or persistence, or laziness.

- *Those which make little difference to your life*, or are relatively unimportant. For example, I have never learned to draw but it doesn't bother me because I have other priorities and little interest. It hardly affects my life at all.

- *Those which are impossible to change*. These must be accepted or circumvented. For example, a person prone to congenital depression can learn to live with it and still have a successful and relatively happy life.

It's important to know which of your so-called weaknesses fall into each category. Then, like Benjamin Franklin, you can develop an active, systematic programme which will lead to steady improvements.

I'm not saying it's easy, but we can all be anything we want to be.

Geoff Thompson

246 Take your list of 'weaknesses' (Section 22) and for each weakness consider:

How would my life improve if I were able overcome this 'weakness' or turn it into a strength? How much better would I feel about myself?

What would be the consequences if I did nothing to change or improve this aspect of myself? What price, if any, would I pay for staying this way?

Use your answers to identify weaknesses which make relatively little difference to you and mark them with a cross.

247 Go through your list from Confidence Builder 246 and underline any that really *cannot* be changed. Then look again – are you sure these can't be changed? Are any merely the result of negative conditioning or unreliable attitudes or beliefs, eg:

- I'm not clever enough.

- No one likes me.

- I'm shy and there's nothing I can do about it.

- I'm too old now. I'm past it.

248 Use this affirmation to help you accept attributes which either you do not wish to change or which *cannot* be changed:

'I accept my... and my... (attributes you will have to learn to live with). This is me, and I'm wonderful, aren't I?'

249 Start working on the attributes you decide are important right away using the ITIA Formula© and Benjamin Franklin approach. Use these affirmations if you feel yourself slipping back:

'I *can* build into myself the qualities and traits of a confident person, and I *will*.'

'Every day in every way I'm becoming more and more confident. Nothing and no one can stop me.'

Display them on your Wall of Confidence.

250 The company you keep is all-important, so surround yourself with supportive friends. Avoid negative, critical, sarcastic people. They'll drag you down if you let them.

251 Write a few notes detailing how you have changed since you started out on this programme and where your priorities lie for the next few weeks.

252 From time to time close your eyes, hold this book in your hands for a few seconds and open it at random. You'll find the information in front of you will be pertinent to some need you have at that moment.

Nothing great is created suddenly, any more than a bunch of grapes or a fig.
If you say to me that you desire a fig, I shall answer, 'that requires time.
Let it first blossom, then bear fruit, then ripen.

Epictetus

Two qualities that are essential for confidence building and a happy and fulfilling life are **patience** and **persistence**. Lasting change takes time, and when the going gets tough remember how much better you feel when you achieved something worthwhile by sticking at it.

So press on. Nothing can take the place of patience and persistence.

Thousands of people have talent.
I might as well congratulate you for having eyes in your head.
The one and only thing that counts is, do you have staying power?

Noel Coward

37 Take a risk

To build confidence you will occasionally have to push yourself to do things you don't feel like doing and put yourself on the line. *Welcome* every opportunity. Avoiding fresh challenges, difficult people and awkward situations is never gratifying in the long term and just keeps you stuck as you are now.

Of course taking risks invites failure, but that's OK. You can't expect to sail through life without coming a cropper sometimes, it's a natural part of human experience. Babies learning to walk topple over many times. As adults we too will fall, recover our balance and get back on our feet again. Nobody gets everything right all the time.

Go on – *take a risk* (you know you want to)! If it feels uncomfortable it's only because you're not used to it. Change always feels uncomfortable at first, because your past conditioning tries to hold on to your old ways. Confident people don't always succeed, but they do always enjoy trying and they don't feel any less a person if they fail.

Be willing to ***confront your fears***. Feel the fear, but don't be affected by it. You don't have to do everything perfectly. Just being yourself and having a go is enough.

Whatever you can do, or dream you can, begin it.
Boldness has genius, magic and power in it.
Begin it now.

Goethe

253 Think about risks you've taken in the past. What happened? How did they work out? Choose three big risks you have taken. What can you learn from them?

254 Think of three things you would love to do, but have been afraid to try because you're unsure of the consequences. For each, write down:

- What would be the best *possible* outcome?
- What would be the *very worst* that could happen?
- What do you most fear?
- How realistic are your fears?

Now do them! Don't be put off, especially by anything others say. You'll probably discover two things: one, your fears were groundless (they often are) and two, you feel terrific!

255 Make this saying (the title of an excellent book by Dr Susan Jeffers) a motto:

'Feel the fear and do it anyway.'

Remind yourself of it whenever you feel unsure of yourself.

256 Relax and let your imagination run wild. Imagine you quit your job at the end of the month.

- What would happen next?

- What effect would it have on your life?

- What will you do?

- What would you like to do? Imagine it becoming reality.

Write down anything significant that comes to mind.

257 Spend a day doing *exactly* what you want to do. Don't compromise. Throughout the day ask, 'What would I like to do right now?' and do it. Keep checking that you're doing exactly what you want.

258 Do something you enjoy, just for you, *every day*, something that inspires you and makes you feel good. If it involves taking a measured risk, so much the better!

259 If your risk requires you to learn new skills, practise them thoroughly. If it involves doing something with others or in front of them, you'll soon discover that once you've mastered them in private you'll have plenty of confidence to display your skills in front of others.

The greatest success is not in never failing,
but in rising every time you fall.

Vince Lombardi

'Now we've done it once, we'd do it again anytime.'

Sisters Valerie and Linda loved singing, but the thought of performing in public terrified them. Humming along to the radio was one thing, but standing up in front of an audience was a different matter. Then one day, encouraged by her daughter's music teacher, Valerie decided to have a go and before long Linda signed up too.

A few weeks later the teacher invited them to take part in a workshop run by a top singing instructor from London, concluding with a concert in front of the other participants plus an invited audience of family and friends.

As the dreaded moment of the performance drew near, they panicked. 'I can't go through with this,' said Valerie to the instructor.

'Neither can I,' added Linda.

'Yes you can' he insisted, pointing. 'You sit on those stools and do it. Now!'

Taken aback by his vehemence they sat down, took a deep breath and began. They sang beautifully and the audience applauded wildly.

'It's amazing how much more confident we feel' they said afterwards. 'Now we've done it once, we know we can do it, and it doesn't feel too bad...'

38 Confidence building activities

The following activities are terrific confidence boosters. Obviously some will appeal to you more than others. For instance, if you enjoy dancing and you're good at it you'll probably feel that taking dancing lessons is unnecessary. But if you hate dancing, lack confidence on the dance floor and find it difficult to express yourself physically, the very idea may traumatise you.

Why do most of us find it hard to put ourselves on the line? Usually because we're frightened of showing ourselves up. But with high self-esteem we don't worry about making fools of ourselves in front of others because we know instinctively that this is not a disaster.

So what if you don't succeed first time? The obstacles don't grow any bigger, but you do! With a positive self-image you can fail completely and *still feel good about yourself.*

- Because I'm OK I can make mistakes. I can fail and still feel good about myself.
- I am enthusiastic about life and filled with energy and purpose.

Failure is the opportunity to begin again, more intelligently.

Henry Ford

260 Join a speakers' club or enrol on a public speaking course. Speaking to an audience is many people's number one fear, but even if you never intend giving a speech, attending speaking classes will do wonders for your confidence.

261 Take singing lessons. Join a choir or small singing group and sing in public. Better still, do it solo. Alternatively, join a drama group.

262 Take dancing lessons – disco, rock 'n' roll, ballroom, it doesn't matter. Use your body. Become more physically expressive. Bear in mind you're not doing it to impress, but to feel more at ease with the way you move. Playing charades with family and friends, or better still, strangers, can bring the same rewards.

263 Take a self-defence course. You get a wonderful feeling of confidence from knowing that you could deal with a physical attack if necessary.

264 If you're shy join a club or society that brings you into contact with others. Choose one that enables you to pursue your favourite hobby or something at which you excel. We all need contact with other people and, no matter how shy you are, you won't cure it by hiding away.

265 Do a bungee jump, absail or go skydiving. Take up rock climbing, hang gliding or white water rafting. Challenging yourself physically is a wonderful way of building confidence.

266 Every evening allow ten minutes to reflect on the day's events. Note the positive aspects of the day. Dwell on the most enjoyable moments as if savouring a delicious morsel of food.

Saturday night failure

Richard was thoroughly miserable. At 35 this successful entrepreneur was still single and lonely. 'I work late most evenings,' he said, 'because I dread going home. There's nothing to go home to.' He had never had a girlfriend, his only sexual contacts being with prostitutes, for which he felt dirty and ashamed.

He believed one of his main problems lay in his inability to join in the dancing at discos and nightclubs. He had been to many down the years, but try as he might was petrified of stepping onto the dance floor. He would stand at the bar watching people dancing and later leaving together, if he stayed that long. Usually he sloped off well before closing time.

Richard was introduced to the ITIA Formula©, encouraged to enrol for dancing lessons, and taught how to use anchoring. In stages he visualised himself arriving at the nightclub, chatting to people and buying drinks, using the 'cool, calm and confident' trigger if he felt his anxiety levels rising. Then he visualised himself calmly stepping onto the dance floor and moving easily – nothing too flamboyant at first – then approaching an attractive woman and dancing with her.

Then he took the plunge. At first he was terrified, but within a few weeks he was able to do everything for which he had set out.

39 Confident body language

When you move confidently and carry your body confidently, you not only feel more confident but others assume that you are.

You may be surprised to learn that only 7% of the information you transmit to others is in the language you use. The remainder comes from:

- 38% How you speak – quality of voice, accent, voice projection, emphasis, expression, pace, volume, pitch etc.

- 55% Body language – posture, position, eye contact, facial expression, head and body movements, gestures, touch etc.

Whereas people often try to disguise their true feelings in their utterances, they communicate them freely through their non-verbals. When your body language tells a different story from your spoken words, guess which is believed? The answer is, *your body language*. It imparts eight times as much information.

Pay more attention to how you use your body. Poor movement and posture restricts breathing, tightens the muscles and brings about skeletal disorders.

One of the best ways of improving your posture is to practise the ***Alexander Technique***, a wonderful method for detecting and releasing muscular tension. It involves moving with the back straight, gaze gently fixed straight ahead, shoulders back but relaxed, ears, shoulders, hips and ankles in line. This has the effect of lengthening and widening the spine giving the lungs a chance to work better. This is the epitome of a confident posture. Moreover, regular practitioners also find themselves mentally calmer and more confident than before.

No one has ever seen a cock crow with its head down.

Alonzo Newton Benn

267 Stand in front of a mirror. Hold your head up, back straight, shoulders back, looking straight ahead. Try to make yourself look bigger, as if you're taking up more space – good posture automatically takes up more space. Now walk briskly and confidently around the room. How do you feel?

A proud, upright stance makes you look more important, even if you're not especially tall. It makes you look younger and slimmer too.

268 Now do the opposite. Droop your shoulders, head down, looking at the floor. Make yourself smaller, as if your body is closing in on itself. How confident do you feel now?

269 Hand and arm movements are very expressive. Learn to use your hands for emphasis, and keep hand movements smooth and flowing. Avoid:

- Folding your arms or wrapping them around yourself (like a cuddle). This indicates a closed, defensive attitude and makes you appear unapproachable.

- Placing your hands in your pockets.

- Tapping on surfaces such as tables and desks with your fingers or on the back of your other hand.

- Fidgeting, scratching, wringing your hands (which shows tension).

- Touching your face or neck. This reveals discomfort or embarrassment.

Become aware of all your mannerisms and gestures. If possible video yourself, watch carefully and make adjustments.

270 Eyes are very expressive.

- Lively, sparkling eyes are attractive. They say, 'Talk to me, I'm approachable.'
- Looking away shows disinterest or deviousness.
- Looking down conveys submission.

Confident people make more frequent eye contact than people who are unsure of themselves, so develop a steady gaze. When you enter a room move around comfortably, smile and make gentle eye contact with everyone; not too much, not too little.

271 Your breathing is very important too. You can calm down instantly and become less tense and anxious by taking your attention to the breath, slowing and deepening it.

Practise calming the breath. Slow breaths and a steady gaze, combined with an anchor such as 'Cool, calm and relaxed', can combat nervousness any time, wherever you are and whoever you're with.

272 Make better use of your personal space. Try to make yourself bigger. The more room you appear to occupy, the more confident and important you appear. But moving too close to others is unsettling, so don't get too near.

273 Try 'steepling'. Join your fingertips to form what looks like a church steeple. This communicates authority and gives the impression you're sure of what you're saying.

A feat of confidence?

Many years ago I was a trainee executive with a large company. As part of my induction I was sent on a presentation skills course. After three days of intensive coaching we all had to make a ten minute presentation, which was to be video-taped, to instructors and colleagues on a subject of our choice.

Well aware of the impression that a wavering voice and incongruent body language made, I practised a clear, steady tone, confident expression and smooth, flowing hand movements in front of a mirror. When the moment arrived, although feeling far from relaxed, I was sure I would *look* and *sound* confident. And so it seemed initially. When the video was played back, my face and upper body looked completely relaxed.

However, the camera operator had noticed something of which I was entirely unaware. He panned in on my feet. Unbeknown to me, but perfectly obvious to everyone else in the room, they were tapping away uncontrollably, with a vigour which would have made Fred Astaire proud!

The moral? If you are not fully confident, no matter how hard you try to disguise it your non-verbals will give you away one way or another.

40 Conditions of worth

The next few sections look at the link between **confidence** and **self-esteem** and your **relationships**. It's two-way:

■ Your relationships with others, both past and present, help determine your confidence.

■ As your confidence and self-esteem grow, your relationships improve.

People lacking in self-esteem often measure their worth in terms of other people's approval. Children and adults alike are under tremendous pressure to earn approval from others by conforming to attitudes and behaviours which are not necessarily of their choosing. This kind of approval is not freely given for *who you are* – it is conditional on *what you do*.

The most common conditions of worth relate to our:

■ **Physical appearance** – including style of dress.

■ **Intelligence** – and mode of speech.

■ **Accomplishments** – sporting, artistic, academic etc.

■ **Money and possessions**.

■ **Family background**.

We all want to be liked by others, and are willing to conform to some extent to win that approval. But when we feel we must do what others want so they'll like us, and this becomes the main reason for our actions, we're in grave danger of giving away our personal power and betraying our deepest values.

Your aim, of course, is to evaluate yourself by your own criteria, knowing that you are not what others think of you, but much more. Now you are an adult the only person whose approval you really need is you.

No one can make you feel inferior without your consent.

Eleanor Roosevelt

274 Think back to your school days. Were you teased or criticised for any of the conditions of worth listed on the previous page? Can you can remember any specific incidents? How did you feel about them at the time?

How do you feel about them now?

275 If you could change six ways in which you believe others see you, what would they be?

276 Do any of your family members, colleagues or friends take pleasure in constantly criticising you and reminding you of your so-called faults? *Ask them to stop.* If this fails, try asking.

'What are you trying to achieve by speaking to me like that?'
or
'Are you trying to make me feel... (stupid, etc)? Well, you've failed.'

277 Write down the very worst thing that can happen if you are rejected by someone. Remember that other people only have the power to upset you if you let them.

278 The reason why many people are so sensitive to conditions of worth imposed on them by others is that they're terrified of *rejection*. They're afraid that others have a poor opinion of them and won't want to know them or, worse, will be openly hostile it they don't conform.

How do you feel about rejection? Write down this sentence:

'The reason why I'm so scared of rejection is…'

Quickly, without thinking about it too hard, write down the first half-dozen reasons that come to mind.

279 Accept that others have the right to say no to your requests, just as you do. But don't take this as a rejection of *you* as a person, nor assume they'll reject *all* your requests.

Remember, the salesperson who wins the most orders is the one who shrugs off the 'no's' and keeps on calling.

280 Accept that it's impossible to please everyone. The sooner you realise this, the better, because then you cease wasting time and energy, physical and emotional, trying to achieve the unachievable. Confident people:

- Know their own minds and live according to their own values.

- Don't necessarily like rejection, but they can cope with it.

- Know you can't control how others think and behave, and don't make themselves unhappy worrying about it.

- Also know that rejection can be a powerful source of learning. You may learn, for example, that certain ways of approaching some people in particular situations work better than others. You always learn more from being rejected than not trying.

The Gestalt Prayer

I do my thing, and you do yours.
I am not in this world to live up to your expectations.
You are not in this world to live up to mine.
I am I, and you are you.
And if by chance we find each other, it's beautiful.
If not, it can't be helped.

The challenge is to be yourself in a world that is trying to make you like everyone else.

Poster spotted in a shop window

41 Give up approval-seeking behaviour

Approval-seeking behaviour implies going along with what you think others expect out of fear that they won't like you. It means being excessively concerned with what others think.

Obviously there is nothing wrong with wanting to be liked and accepted; it's a natural human desire. But it becomes a problem when you allow others' approval to dictate how you feel about yourself. Psychologists recognise this as a deep-seated neurosis.

Approval-seeking behaviour does have short-term benefits; it keeps others happy, gets them off your back. But it could be at the expense of your long-term self-esteem. You cannot find long-term happiness by constantly pandering to others. Besides, people soon tire of a 'yes-man'.

There is only one person whose approval you really *need*, and that's *you*. Other people's expectations are not your concern. You didn't create them, and you don't own them. If others don't like what you do that's their problem, not yours.

When you stop doing things just because others expect it, the sense of freedom can be exhilarating. No longer do you have to pretend to be something you're not. You always have the choice of how to respond to others' expectations. Use it wisely!

We can secure other people's approval if we do right and try hard, but our own is worth a hundred of it.

Mark Twain

281

Which if any of these are typical of you?

- Constantly craving recognition from others.

- Comparing yourself unfavourably with others.

- Being daunted by someone else's success.

- Being over generous to try to get others to like you.

- Not applying for a promotion because you don't believe you're up to the job.

- A tendency to seek out others who are shy or have low self esteem.

- Feeling like a victim most of the time.

- Frequently making excuses to avoid social events, or simply not turning up.

- Crossing the road or hiding to avoid speaking to someone.

- Staying in the background, for instance by avoiding wearing bright clothes or staying quiet when you've got something to say.

If you've answered yes to any of the above, what does this say about you? What changes do you intend to make?

282

If you ever catch yourself thinking 'What would so and so think?', ' If I do or say this, what will people say?' or similar thoughts, *change them*. They reveal a desperate need for approval. Immediately substitute them with the affirmation:

'I am my own person.'

283 Use this affirmation whenever you feel pressured, angered or irritated by another person:

'I do not allow anyone else's words or behaviour to spoil my day.'

284 It is essential to realise that *you won't get on with everyone.* To think otherwise is unrealistic, encourages approval-seeking behaviour, and inevitably damages your self-esteem.

There are some people with whom you enjoy a mutual liking and who become firm friends. You will also meet people with whom you have little in common, but can maintain polite and friendly relationships. But it is also inevitable that you will meet people with whom you will never see eye to eye, who dislike you and you them. You may as well accept that they don't like you and just try to remain calm and courteous in their presence.

285 Expect your share of disapproval. Even your best friends don't approve of you all of the time! Accept that you won't win over everyone you meet. And stop worrying: life is not a popularity contest!

286 If you find yourself conforming for the sake of it, which implies that you are allowing others to make your decisions for you, ask yourself, 'Why am I doing this? Do I really want to? Or is it just because someone else expects it?'

Listen to your inner self and follow your intuition. Then if you decide to comply it is *your* choice.

287 Don't rebel for the sake of it either: you're still judging yourself by others' criteria and not necessarily being true to yourself. *You* must decide what you believe in and how you conduct yourself.

What would the teacher think?

Patricia was a worrier, and the thing she worried about most was what others thought of her. One day her son's teacher asked the class to take some newspapers to school the following day. All she could find at first was last week's local free advertiser and a copy of a down-market tabloid known mainly for the page displaying pictures of topless women. Patricia went into a panic. She couldn't let him take either of those. What would the teacher think?

Eventually, after a lengthy and heated discussion with her husband, he popped round to the next door neighbour's and returned with a few spare copies of a quality broadsheet. Phew!

In the event the teacher didn't even look at the newspaper. She only wanted them for papier mache!

42 First impressions

First impressions last. We make up our minds about other people very quickly. We form 90% of our opinions about others in the first four minutes, so it's vital you think about how you present yourself to others.

The next few sections are about *communicating with others*. Talking to other people can be a nightmare when you lack confidence, especially if you're meeting them for the first time. But even though we don't tend to think of it that way, **conversation** is a skill we can all learn, starting with a few basic techniques, then gradually developing our own style.

A sustained effort to improve your **listening**, **conversational skills** and **assertiveness** will enable you to reach new heights of confidence. Nothing brings confidence more surely than knowing that you can talk to people easily; that you always have something to say and know how to say it.

We often pardon those who bore us, but never those whom we bore.

Duc De La Rochefoucauld

---

288 Write a short paragraph (100 words maximum) of introduction about yourself, using only positive words and phrases. Memorise it. Stand in front of a mirror and read it as if you were introducing yourself to an audience of strangers. It should take no longer than 30 seconds. How does it sound? How do you feel?

---

289 When you meet someone for the first time their initial impression of you is visual – your appearance and body language.

- Your face is the most expressive part of your body, so smile. Smiling is friendly, communicates warmth, is attractive, and says more than words ever could.

- Use gentle, flowing hand movements.

- Develop a firm handshake. A limp handshake suggests a weak character.

---

290 Practise getting into rapport with others quickly, discovering what you have in common. Get them to talk about themselves and their interests and appeal to their need for approval. Affectionately comment on what you appreciate about them. Ask about their family, their work, hobbies and leisure interests, holidays, interests and education. Listen patiently to their reply. Avoid contentious topics such as politics, sex and religion until you know them better.

291 Initiate a conversation with at least one new person every day. If you're nervous practise deep breathing and quick relaxers beforehand. If it doesn't go well to start with don't panic: learn from it, try again and persevere.

292 Practise using open-ended questions to initiate conversations, check that you've heard the other person correctly and keep conversations going. *Closed* questions require only a yes, no or don't know answer, which swiftly brings the conversation to a close. *Open-ended* questions encourage others to speak. For example, asking 'Are you happy?' is a conversation killer, but 'You look happy – what's been happening to you?' demands a fuller response. Use open-ended questions and prompts such as:

- How do you mean?
- Tell me more about...
- Why do you say that?
- How do you feel about...?
- What do you think of...?

293 Develop a pleasing and confident tone of voice. Talk unhurriedly with a steady, clear tone of voice and breathe slowly as you speak.

- Vary the tone, pace and pitch of your voice. This makes your conversation sound more interesting.
- Pitch your voice in the middle range. Nervous people pitch their voices too high.
- Your tone of voice conveys emotion. Aim for a warm, mellow tone.
- Don't speak too fast or too slowly. Too fast and you come across as over-excited or tense. Too slowly is boring.

Speak into a tape recorder. How do you sound? Few people like the sound of their voice on tape, but remember, what you hear is *how you actually come across* to others.

294

If you're part of a group who are mocking or criticising others, or making cruel comparisons, don't get involved. Stay quiet and you'll experience a wonderful sense of freedom. Gossip is like a boomerang – it always returns to hurt you.

Keep your options open!

There was a buzz in the hall as the new graduates and their parents consulted the seating plan and made their way to the tables. The ceremony had gone well. Now they could relax and tuck into a sumptuous graduation dinner in these stately surroundings.

But not everyone. The morning had been something of a trial for Will, a shy, retiring man who nevertheless enjoyed company. He turned to the woman next to him, anxious to start a conversation. He smiled nervously, trying to think of something witty to say. 'I've always thought it's important to keep two things open in life,' he blurted out, 'your options and your bowels.'

There was an embarrassed silence around the table, followed by uneasy spluttering. The woman turned her back. Will's daughter blushed. And no further attempts at conversation ensued for the remainder of the lunch.

Two people-pleasing attitudes:

■ A stranger is simply a friend I've only just met.

■ I'll make everyone glad they met me.

43 Be a good listener

The art of good communication can be summarised in four points:

- **Be a good listener** so you truly understand what others say to you. Good listening earns genuine respect and admiration, and is one of the secrets of popularity.

- **Have something good to say**. Boring people make boring conversation.

- **Express yourself well**. Use colourful, descriptive language. Make your conversation sound interesting.

- **Appeal to the emotions**. There's a wise saying: The head never hears until the heart has listened.

You'd be amazed how much more confident you feel when you're a good listener. You find you can handle business and social situations confidently. Become a good listener and you'll gain a reputation as a good conversationalist without having to say very much at all.

The Chinese verb to listen is composed of five characters meaning ear, you, eyes, individual attention, heart. The art of listening involves all of our being.

Lynda Field

295 Commit to becoming a better listener. Real listening means taking the time and trouble to grasp what is being said to you and reflecting back that understanding. When someone speaks to you, if safe stop what you're doing and patiently focus your full attention on them. Observe their facial expression and body language. Take responsibility for making sure you fully understand.

296 It's not enough to listen carefully – you must also *show* that you are listening. Use the mnemonic SOFTEN:

- **Smile**.

- Adopt an **open posture** with uncrossed arms and legs.

- Lean **forward** and **face** them squarely.

- Use **touch** where appropriate.

- Make **eye** contact – not too much; up to three or four seconds at a time.

- **Nod** your head to signify understanding and/or approval.

Do all this in a non-threatening manner. For example, a light touch and a little eye contact communicate warmth and support, but too much could be misinterpreted.

297 If you catch yourself interrupting stop immediately, apologise, and invite the other person to continue.

298 Don't give the impression that you're just waiting for a pause so that you can jump in. A conversation was once described as 'two people waiting for the other to stop speaking so they can start talking.'

There is often a temptation to use listening time to rehearse your reply. If you have a tendency to do this, try the following. When the speaker stops talking, count to three before replying. Then you know they really have finished, and are not just pausing to take a breath.

299 Check that you've heard and understood accurately by giving feedback. Precis what you've heard. For example:

'If I understand you correctly, you're saying…'

or

'So you think…?'

The speaker will soon correct you if you've misunderstood.

300 Learn to read non-verbals. Remember, body language imparts eight times as much information as words, and tone of voice five times as much. Where verbals and non-verbals contradict each other, believe the non-verbals.

301 Good listening doesn't mean agreeing if you don't like what you're hearing. If you disagree you're perfectly at liberty to say so. You can *accept* another's views without *sharing* them, so be aware that it's all right to agree to differ.

You don't have to be a sheep to be popular. People are instinctively drawn to someone who has strength of character and a mind of their own.

'So glad I'd listened'

A client told me this story.

'I was travelling home on a bus when an elderly man, stinking of alcohol, sat down beside me, a bit too close for my liking. My first instinct was to move to another seat, which is what I would normally have done, but the bus was crowded and I didn't want to appear rude. I felt extremely uncomfortable.

The man started talking to me. At first I listened. He seemed harmless enough, so I decided to ask some open-ended questions to see if I could keep the conversation going. I noticed he had several carrier bags with him, and asked him if he enjoyed shopping. He said he didn't particularly, but since his wife died several years ago he had no choice. I asked about his wife, and he told me how much he missed her. They had known each other at school, married young and been together for nearly half a century. He had got into the habit of having a few drinks with his friends on the way home from town to delay going back to an empty house. He seemed glad to have an opportunity to talk about his wife, and wished me a cheery goodbye when he reached his stop.

As he rose from his seat, he said he'd enjoyed our conversation, but I was aware I hadn't really said very much. I was glad I had listened to him. *And I noticed my uncomfortable feelings had gone completely.*'

44 Stand up for yourself

Standing up for yourself – *assertiveness* – means expressing yourself clearly, staying true to your needs and values, while at the same time respecting the dignity of others.

Assertiveness is not to be confused with arrogance, rudeness and being unrealistic in your expectations of others. Confident, well-adjusted people have no need to brag, or be overbearing.

When you know how to stand up for yourself you deal with situations, including the most difficult, effectively. You are unlikely to be steamrollered into anything against your will.

Remember, *you get treated the way you teach others to treat you.* Assert yourself and you gain others' respect. Your relationships are more sincere, because everyone understands you perfectly.

Too often our behaviour is dictated by obligation to others; in the process, we forget the primary obligation: to be ourselves.

Arthur Miller

302 Think about times in the past when you have not stood up for yourself. How do you wish you'd handled them? How could you respond more assertively if something similar happened again?

303 Make a list of the benefits *to you personally* of becoming more assertive. Then make a list of the disadvantages of staying as you are.

304 In which areas of your life would you like to be more assertive: at work, at home, in social activities, etc? Do you allow yourself to be pushed around?

305 Just for today don't say anything that conflicts with your true feelings, wishes, needs and values. Be firm and polite at all times, but don't allow anyone to take advantage of you.

At the end of the day, reflect. How well did it go? Learn from it, then do the same again tomorrow.

306 When you're unhappy about something, how do you normally express it?

1. Let people know in a roundabout way, eg by dropping hints or going into a bad mood?

2. Keep quiet for fear of causing a scene or upsetting others?

3. Say how you feel and be specific?

4. Lose your temper or look for someone to blame?

307 (2) above describes *passive* behaviour. Passivity stems from lack of confidence.

If you're a passive person, what is it about you that makes others treat you as they do? Write down your thoughts, and affirm that you intend to break away from submissive behaviour and become more assertive.

308 (1) and (4) in Confidence Builder 306 describe aggressive behaviour. Aggressive people don't mind taking advantage of others and take little account of their feelings. They believe aggression is the only way to get what they want.

Aggression is often a smokescreen used by insecure people to hide their insecurities. They actually lack confidence, but don't admit it. They use fear and guilt to manipulate people, either by being loud and intimidating or, just as reprehensible, using subtle put-downs, sarcasm and emotional blackmail.

Confident people have no need to abuse, exploit or humiliate others less self-assured than themselves. Big egos do not equate to high self-esteem.

A few words of advice

We get used to knowing a person in a certain way. As you become more confident there will be those who don't like the change; they may even feel threatened by it. And others may take a while to adjust.

But don't let this deter you. They're not thinking of you. They're projecting their lack of self-esteem on to you. The last thing you'll want is to be knocked back to where you were. And why should you be? Just be sensitive to their feelings until they've become used to the new you.

You may even have to be prepared to lose a few friends and seek out more support-ive relationships. But this won't be a problem. True friends will be pleased to see the positive changes you're making.

45 How to be assertive

Even if you've never considered yourself to be assertive, mastering a few basic techniques soon starts to reap untold rewards. Apply the ITIA Formula©:

- **Decide** to become more assertive.

- **Think** like an assertive person, and think of yourself as one.

- **Imagine** yourself behaving assertively and being treated accordingly.

- **Act** assertively. Start by taking small steps. Keep going until the uncomfortable feelings fade.

This above all: to thine own self be true. And it must follow, as the night the day, thou canst not then be false to any man.

William Shakespeare

309 Use these affirmations:

> 'I think, speak and act assertively at all times.'
> 'I used to be passive, but all that is changing.
> I am becoming more assertive every day.'

310 Mentally rehearse potentially difficult situations. 'Imagine' and 'feel' yourself handling them assertively. 'See' others responding accordingly.

311 Practise assertive non-verbals. Be aware of the non-verbal signals you give out:

- Talk unhurriedly, with a clear, steady tone.
- Make a habit of taking slightly more time to reply.
- Give relaxed eye contact: not too much, not too little.
- Avoid fidgeting, scratching, and touching your hair and face.

312 Make your point clearly, with conviction, and don't waffle. Then shut up. If you don't succeed straight away, say it again, and if necessary keep repeating it. Change the wording if you wish, but not the message. Stay calm and don't allow yourself to be sidetracked.

313 If someone upsets or angers you, comment on the offending *behaviour*. Attacking a person's *character* merely gets their back up and makes it less likely they will listen to you. Say how you have been affected, and what you would like to happen next. For example:

'I don't like it when you... It makes me feel... And if it continues/ you don't stop, these will be the consequences. I want you to...'

Example: 'I don't like it when you talk about my friend like that. It makes me feel as if I can't trust you. If you don't stop it, I'll tell her what you said. I want you to promise me you won't do it again.'

314 The best strategy to deal with aggressive behaviour is to challenge it *immediately*. When confronted aggressors often accuse you of being oversensitive or letting your imagination run away with you, but sometimes they're genuinely unaware of how they're coming across and taken aback by your comment. Say:

'You're not trying to make me feel... are you?'
'You're not trying to... (hurt, frighten, control etc.) me, are you?'

If they try it on again, *keep challenging*. They won't like it, but sooner or later they'll get the point.

315 Sign up for an assertiveness course. Make sure it offers plenty of opportunity to practise with other people. If this is not possible, buy an eduactional video or set of audio tapes on assertiveness, *and apply it!*

Choose 'kind'

Truly assertive people use their skills responsibly. They know when to 'chill out' and when to 'come on strong'. And they never deliberately hurt others' feelings.

So whenever you're faced with a choice of demonstrating how right you are and simply being kind, ask yourself whether it really matters, and if it doesn't, *choose kind!*

An assertive response

If someone is rude to you, put a hurt expression on your face and say, 'You know, I found that *awfully* rude!'

46 Say no when you mean no

Assertive people find it easy to say no when they mean no. They don't worry about being seen in a bad light. They know that just because they've been asked doesn't mean they're under any obligation. Passive people, on the other hand, usually find it hard to refuse.

Say you're asked a favour. It's inconvenient. You'd like to say no.

- **Passive behaviour:** Saying, 'yes' while thinking, 'What a nuisance. Oh well!' or making a string of half-hearted excuses in a feeble attempt to avoid causing offence.

- **Aggressive behaviour:** A blunt response, probably while thinking, 'Why the … should I?'

- **Assertive behaviour:** A warm, friendly smile, while saying, 'No, I'm sorry it's not convenient. I've made other arrangements'.

In the long run saying yes when you don't mean it only makes things worse for yourself. It puts you at greater risk of stress and lowers your confidence and self-respect.

> *If we want to feet truly confident, we must break the habit of trying to please all people, all of the time*
>
> **Gael Lindenfield**

316

Think of all the things you have done with or for other people this past week. Go through the list one by one. Did you:

- Initiate this activity?

- Happily go along with someone else's suggestion?

- Passively comply against your better judgement or wishes?

317

Just for today say no to all requests made of you unless, of course, it's something you especially want to do. Then do the same again tomorrow. And the day after...

318

Practise saying no clearly and unambiguously whenever a suitable opportunity arises. Get used to hearing yourself saying it. Smile. Use a pleasant tone of voice and warm, open body language to show the other person you aren't just being unpleasant. If you like, soften your reply so as not to offend. For instance:

- 'I'd prefer not to...'

- 'That' s a great idea, but I'm not interested at present.'

- 'I'm sorry to hear about your problem, but I'm not able to help at the moment.'

Don't feel obliged to justify your decision.

319 Choose a scenario such as being invited to a party to which you don't want to go, and mentally rehearse yourself turning it down.

320 Don't let others burden you with their problems unless you genuinely wish to get involved. Know where the boundaries lie. Let them know firmly and clearly that you won't go along with their request.

321 Always make it clear that you are turning down the *request*, not rejecting the *person*. One way is to pay a compliment before refusing. eg 'I really admire the work you do, but I don't wish to make a donation to your charity at this time.'

322 At times there's no way round it – you just have to say no and keep saying no until they've got the message.

*The important thing is not what they think
of me; it is what I think of them.*

Queen Victoria

People lacking in confidence are often tempted to duck and weave when others try to talk them round to their point of view.

- Paul loves expressing an opinion but feels anxious if anyone disagrees with him, so he hedges his bets as much as possible by making sure his ideas will be acceptable to the person to whom he's talking at any time.

- Bert was once sold a set of encyclopaedias at the door because he didn't want to upset the salesman.

- Jennifer has a wardrobe full of clothes she has never worn because she is too timid to resist the attentions of persuasive shop assistants.

- John, aged 49, spends Sunday afternoons at his mother's, despite his children's protestations, because she expects it and he is too timid to tell her that some weeks he would rather make other arrangements.

47 Compliments and criticisms

Wouldn't it be wonderful to go through life without ever being criticised? Perhaps, but this is not possible. Employers, spouses, children, parents, friends and colleagues will all criticise you from time to time. You probably can't stop them, but you can learn to handle it.

Your attitude to criticism is heavily influenced by your experiences as a child; critical parents tend to raise either critical or defensive children. Only those with very low opinions of themselves are easily hurt or embarrassed by criticism, but *if you have confidence in yourself you aren't unduly worried by it.* You realise that people who constantly criticise others usually feel bad about themselves, and are projecting their low self-esteem onto others.

The inability to accept a compliment is another sign of low self-esteem. People lacking in confidence often regard compliments with suspicion, wondering why the other person is being so nice and if there's an ulterior motive. *Get comfortable with compliments.* They make both the giver and receiver feel good and build the self-esteem of all concerned.

What you think of me is none of my business.

Terry Cole-Whittaker

323 Ask yourself, how do you respond to criticism. How do you feel when someone criticises you? How do you feel when you know you are about to be criticised? Do you have any 'crumble buttons' – highly sensitive areas which immediately trigger strong defensive feelings in you? Do you know where they come from?

Unless you're aware of your vulnerable areas others may pick up on them and use them to deliberately embarrass or belittle you.

324 When someone criticises you, before you react try to ascertain why they are doing so and whether the criticism is fair. If it is false firmly reject it using your assertiveness skills.

But if you feel they have your best interests at heart and that they are making a fair point, thank them and learn from it. And be willing to admit your mistakes and apologise if appropriate. It takes confidence and high self-esteem to admit you're wrong.

325 Do you often find yourself being critical of others?

If so, why do you think that is?

326 If you need to criticise:

- Choose the time and place carefully so they'll be receptive to your comments.
- Don't criticise in front of others; you wouldn't like it, and neither will they.
- Criticise their conduct, not their character, and give examples of the behaviour you're criticising.
- Don't label them: avoid insults and put-downs such as lazy, stupid, ignorant etc.

327 Use the critical sandwich. Start with a positive, then make your criticism. Finish with a constructive remark.

For example, 'As you know, I've been extremely happy with your work since you joined us, but there is one thing I need to mention. I've noticed you're getting in later and later each morning: you were half an hour late yesterday, and 20 minutes late on Tuesday. Now I know the buses haven't been all that reliable recently, but please make an effort to be punctual. So please, carry on with the good work. It's good to have you on our team.'

328 Pay compliments often. The secret of giving a compliment is to pick the right moment, keep it short and then shut up. Be sincere – most people can spot empty flattery a mile off.

When you pay a compliment, don't put yourself down. The sentence in italics below is unnecessary and sends an awful message to the subconscious Prover:

'I was impressed by the way you dealt with the problem. *I couldn't have done it so well.*'

329 When someone pays you a compliment, smile and say, 'Thank you', or 'How kind of you.' That's all you need to do. Not only will you feel good, but you are showing respect to the giver too.

Comfortable with compliments

I overheard this clumsy attempt to give and receive a compliment at a recent talk on confidence. The presenter had asked the audience to compliment the person next to them. A middle-aged man turned to the young woman to his right.

'You're friendly,' he said, 'you remind me of my daughter.'

She blushed. 'But your daughter might not be very nice,' she replied. He turned away, speechless.

48 How to ask for what you want

Many people find it difficult to ask for what they want or to complain about poor service even when they are fully justified. They think it' s impolite. They don't like upsetting people, or worry they might be met with hostility. They prefer to 'put up and shut up'. Why? There are two main root causes:

- **Low self-esteem**; feeling unworthy of getting what they want.
- Not knowing how to **ask or complain effectively**.

Confident people aren't afraid to complain. They're happy to ask for help when they need it. They find out *what they're entitled to*, and refuse to settle for any less. They know it's better to ask and run the risk of being turned down than to bottle up their grievances and lose out for sure.

The greatest danger for most of us is not that our aim is too high and we miss it, but that it is too low and we reach it.

Michelangelo

330

Next time you feel like chickening out of asking for something for fear of looking stupid or provoking an angry reaction, ask yourself these three questions:

- What's the worst thing that could happen?

- Could I handle it? (Tell yourself 'yes!')

- What's the best strategy?

Then ignore your fears, go ahead and ask anyway!

331

Make a list of requests you would like to make of other people. For example, would you like to ask your boss for a raise? Is there anyone you would like to ask for a date? Take the top three or four requests. Work out what you' re going to say beforehand. Mentally rehearse yourself making the request and it being granted. Then go and do it!

332

When you ask, first be clear of exactly what you want. Then:

- Ask with the firm expectation that you will succeed.

- Don't beat around the bush. Start with 'I want' or 'I would like'.

- Avoid apologetic phrases like: 'I'm afraid' and 'I'm sorry but...'

- Don't be sidetracked.

If you like, soften your request with a phrase such as 'I realise this may be a little inconvenient, but...', making sure that your body language shows that you expect to have your demand met.

333 When complaining:

- Complain to the right person, one who has the authority to put things right.
- State what you want clearly. Don't be embarrassed.
- Stay calm and in control. Don't make idle threats.
- Ask for the names of the people to whom you complain.

334 Sometimes it is better to ask for information or make a suggestion rather than make an outright demand. For example, try these:

- 'What would it take for you to (state your requirement)?'
- 'What do you normally do in these circumstances?'
- 'May I make a suggestion. Why don't you...?'
- 'What do I have to do to qualify for a refund?'

Once you know their rules and procedures, you can use them to your advantage.

335 If your request or complaint is refused, calmly repeat it as many times as necessary, without losing sight of what you want. Try:

- 'You may not have heard me but...'
- 'Please listen while I say it again...'
- 'But the point is...'
- 'I realise that... but I still want...'

If you still don't get what you want, learn from the experience and try a different approach next time.

336 Be gracious. When you've got what you want, say 'thank you' to everyone concerned.

'You didn't ask!'

Many years ago, before I was as confident as I am now, our camper van broke down in Germany. The insurers arranged for us to be towed to a local garage. We were told we could camp on the spare ground behind the garage while repairs were carried out and use the forecourt facilities during trading hours.

My wife, three young children and I stayed there for three days and nights, with no running water and no toilets from 6pm to 8am, no privacy, and constant noise from the busy road.

By the fourth day we were very fed up. Repairs hadn't even started because they couldn't get spare parts, so we telephoned the insurance company in England. 'This is intolerable,' we said. 'At this rate we could be here for days. What can we do?'

'Your policy entitles you to bed and breakfast in a three star hotel until your van is repaired,' the young woman on the 'phone informed us. 'Do you want us to arrange it for you? We'll fix it up right away.'

Astonished, we asked why no one had told us this before. 'You didn't ask!' she replied.

Would you believe it! We'd spent three days and nights living on a mud patch when we could have been staying in a comfortable hotel! All because we had been reluctant to ask about our entitlement.

49 Lighten up

People who lack confidence often take themselves very seriously. They take offence easily and quickly get defensive. They rise to the bait when someone pokes fun at them (and they do make easy targets). You can easily spot such people – they're usually on their own!

It's impossible to laugh and feel anxious at the same time, and the less anxious, the more confident you feel. *So lighten up.* Make a determined effort to see the funny side of life. Seek out people who have a good sense of humour, and have one or two funny stories up your sleeve.

When you laugh and make others laugh, it does wonders for your self-esteem.

Angels fly because they take themselves lightly.

Alan Watts

---

337 For the next few days step back and observe your interactions with others. How often do you:

- Over-analyse?

- Talk about yourself and/or your problems?

- Sulk?

- Miss seeing the funny side of situations?

- Say 'I'?

- Take offence?

If you answered 'often' to any of these, you need to lighten up.

---

338 Take every opportunity to have a good laugh. Watch funny films and videos. Read comic books. Listen to comedy programmes on the radio, cassette tape or CD. When things don't go your way, smile, and ask yourself:

'What's funny about this that I never noticed before?'

---

339 Three things to avoid:

- Giggling: this betrays nervousness.

- 'Isn't it awful' conversations: they focus your attention on what you *don't* want.

- Cheap laughs at other people's expense. Confident people are never sarcastic or unkind. They don't need to be.

340 Do you get into lots of arguments? Try a different approach. If someone expresses an opinion you don't share:

1. Decide whether it's important enough to raise your objection. It usually isn't.

2. Say, 'You could be right about that.'

3. Leave it at that. Either change the subject or move away.

Confident people don't feel they have to prove they're right all the time. They cheerfully accept that others may hold a different point of view. As Lao-Tsu said, *'One who is too insistent on his own views finds few to agree with him.'*

341 If you feel under attack from another person, just say to yourself, 'Shields up!' and imagine an invisible energy force surrounding you. (Fans of science fiction programmes such as *Star Trek*, know exactly what I mean.) The imaginary field-force is a powerful form of psychic protection.

342 Music alters mood. When you want to feet relaxed, listen to relaxing music. When you want to be inspired, inspiring music; energised, rousing music; confident, music that excites, revitalises and cheers you.

343 Make confidence-building fun. Every time you smash through a barrier or overcome a new hurdle, reward yourself. Do something you enjoy, that encourages you, that makes you want to carry on growing.

Whoever makes you laugh helps you live.

Menander

Michael was one of the most intense young men I have ever met. Still living with his parents at 28, he had no social life and had never had a girlfriend. 'Why would any girl want to talk to me?' he asked me.

Within two minutes of meeting him the reason was obvious. He had no apparent sense of humour. The only TV programmes he watched were documentaries, and he couldn't name a single comedian who made him laugh. When he met people he was so eager to show off his immense knowledge that they soon switched off. He thought that sharing his problems would make women sympathetic, but it merely drove them away. Then he would take offence at their 'rudeness' and go into a sulk.

Michael was in therapy for several months, during which he learned, among other things, to use the ITIA Formula©, find a purpose and cultivate some social skills. But the biggest breakthrough came when he realised his serious demeanour put people off. He immediately resolved to lighten up and the change over the following weeks was remarkable.

A few months after he concluded therapy a postcard arrived from Egypt. He had quit his job and set off on a world tour with his new girlfriend. The following year he sent cards from India, Malaysia, Australia, New Zealand, and South and North America.

I have no idea where he is now or what he's doing, but I imagine it's a lot of fun!

50 Emotional intelligence

Emotional intelligence is central for high self-esteem, confidence and assertiveness. It has two aspects, which are equally important:

- **Self-awareness:** an understanding of, and ability to manage your emotions.
- The ability to **sense what others feel** and respond appropriately. People who have this communicate more effectively, make friends more easily and inspire loyalty and confidence.

Human beings are more inclined to act emotionally than logically. When you relate to others on an *emotional* level, and realise that they're unlikely to think, feel and react like you – you get on better with everybody. Be sensitive to others' feelings, accept and empathise with them. Then you'll be more confident in all your personal interactions.

Grant me the serenity to accept the things I cannot change, Courage to change the things which should be changed, And the wisdom to know the difference,

Reinhold Niebuhr

344 Reflect on what you learned about emotions from the adults in your life when you were a child. Take this sentence and fill in the gaps:

'Because of what happened when...,
I am likely to start feeling... when... Perhaps that's why…'

For example 'Because Mum and Dad were always arguing when I was a child, I am likely to start feeling nervous when people raise their voices. Perhaps that's why I prefer to avoid confrontation.'

345 Own your emotions: *they all originate inside you.* They are your response to what you perceive and believe about what happens around you. People frequently make statements like, 'My husband annoyed me', 'You're winding me up' or 'You're p****g me off,' but there's no real validity to any of them. Others can trigger emotional responses, but they can't *make* you feel anything. You and you alone create your emotions.

It would be more correct to say, 'My husband's behaviour triggered a response of annoyance in me.' 'I am responding to your behaviour with a feeling of irritation.'

Accepting full responsibility for your emotions is the basis of emotional intelligence.

346

Feelings can be triggered subconsciously by countless factors beyond your control – it's the way you're made. But you don' t have to be governed by them. Haven't you overruled your emotions when you knew that acting on them would have had disastrous consequences? For instance, when you've been so angry with someone you wanted to hit them, but restrained yourself.

Think of five or six instances when you felt yourself becoming emotional (eg angry, jealous, afraid) and didn't act on it. What happened? How did you handle it? What was the outcome? What would have happened if you'd gone with the emotion?

347

You can be grossly misled by your emotions.

- Just because something *feels* wrong, it doesn't necessarily follow that it *is* wrong.

- Similarly, just because it *feels* right, it doesn't automatically follow that it *is* right.

Millions are terrified of domestic spiders; but these tiny creatures carry no threat. These poor unfortunate people are being tricked by their own senses!

When an anxious feeling comes over you, ask yourself, 'Where is this coming from? Am I really in danger? Or am I merely being deceived by my emotional conditioning?'

348

Try not to identify with your emotions. They are something you experience, but they are not you. Train yourself to watch them as if they were happening to someone else. Be curious about them, allow them to be, *but don't react.*

When you stay calm and simply observe an emotion without reacting, healing takes place. You still feel it, *but you're no longer affected by it.*

349 There's an intimate connection between your breathing and emotional state. When you breathe slowly and deeply, anxiety and irritability melt away. Try it! Breathe slowly and deeply for two minutes. Then make your breathing rapid and shallow for two minutes. How do you feel?

Whenever you want to take charge of your emotions, take your awareness to your breathing. Take a long, slow breath and let out a loud extended sigh. Breathe slowly and evenly for a few minutes. You'll definitely feel calmer.

350 Don't try to suppress your emotions – in the long term, this intensifies them. Sooner or later you *will* have to face up to them.

Don't deliberately avoid situations which bring discomfort, for instance making excuses to stay away from a party because of shyness, or refusing to apply for a promotion for fear of the interview. Avoidance temporarily dulls the pain, but also eliminates any possibility of having emotions you *would* like – fun, friendship, adventure and so on. It's not much fun staying at home when you know your friends are out enjoying themselves, or watching others less able than yourself leapfrogging over you at work.

Face up to your emotions rather than run away from them, learn to handle them more appropriately, and their effect on you soon diminishes.

51 Take an interest in others

One of the great secrets of building confidence and self-esteem is to become *less self-centred*. Self-absorbed people rarely feel good about themselves.

■ Take an active interest in others.

■ When you focus your attention on others rather than yourself, you make them feel better and raise their self-esteem.

■ And every time you contribute to raising another's self-esteem, you simultaneously raise your own to at least the same degree.

In the words of Og Mandino, 'Happiness is a perfume you cannot pour on others without getting a few drops on yourself.'

When we seek to discover the best in others,
we somehow bring out the best in ourselves.

William Arthur Ward

351
Aim to do something to help raise the self-esteem of at least three other people every day. This doesn't require a great deal of time and effort, just a little thought. Simply giving someone your undivided attention makes them feel more valued and important.

Start with those closest to you – your family and friends. Three a day adds up to over 1,000 acts of kindness in the course of a year – a valuable contribution to others' happiness.

352
The golden rule which underpins all relationships is 'Do unto others as you would have them do unto you'. Follow this, and you not only make others feel better about themselves, but you also find you make many friends.

Begin applying the golden rule by thinking about what you are about to say *before* you open your mouth. Ask yourself, 'How would I feel if someone did or said this to me?'

353 Embrace every opportunity to offer a kind word or compliment. It costs nothing, yet brings so much benefit to both the recipient and giver:

- Say thank you often.

- Sincerely praise others' kindness, honesty, generosity, etc.

- Plant a suggestion in their minds that they <u>can</u> succeed.

- Avoid blame, ridicule, moralising and sarcasm.

- Only criticise where necessary, and do it constructively. Thoughtless criticism destroys self-confidence. We do the best we can most of the time and it hurts when our efforts are belittled.

354 Stop worrying about the impression you are making and focus on others instead. Most people are too preoccupied with themselves to take much notice of you. When you walk into a room, stop thinking, 'Everyone's looking at me, I wonder what they think of me?' Instead think, 'What an interesting group of people. I wonder what kind of lives they lead!'

355 Accept people as they are. Confident people are happy for others to be themselves. They don't try to control them – they don't need to. They allow them to think for themselves and make their own decisions. Trying to change others leads only to resistance and resentment on both sides. They're not going to change for you unless *they* want to, any more than you'd change for them.

Here's a powerful affirmation:

'I gladly and willingly accept everybody exactly as they are.'

356 Go through the next 24 hours without judging anyone. If you succeed, congratulate yourself, then do the same the following day. If you don't quite manage it, try again. Keep trying until it becomes a permanent habit.

357 Constantly look for ways to help others. Practise spontaneous acts of kindness. Do something unexpected for a stranger for no logical reason at all. This not only makes you feel good about yourself and provides a genuine service to someone else, but it also reminds you of the most important things in life (love and kindness).

Love and service

We feel better about ourselves when we concentrate on giving rather than receiving, and when we show consideration for others spreading love and happiness in every way we can. Whenever we give to others they feel valued, and it doesn't have to be much. Even a smile, a kind word and a few moments of our time are precious gifts.

Not only do we feel good about ourselves when we help others, but there's a knock-on effect. And we never know how far it will go. A few years ago I helped a young musician overcome stage fright. She couldn't afford the treatment so I waived my fee. At the time I was planning a new audio programme and it turned out that her father owned a recording studio. He was so grateful to me for helping his daughter that he offered the use of his studio at a very reasonable rate.

Get your mind off 'What's in it for me?' and ask instead, 'What can I do for you?'

52 Choose peace

Deep inside, at our very core, lies a natural centre of absolute stillness and peace which can bring a profound sense of wellbeing. This is the spiritual self – but how do we get in touch with it and experience it in our daily lives?

It starts by appreciating who and what we really are – that, in the words of Pierre de Chardin, *'We are not human beings having spiritual experiences, but spiritual beings having human experiences.'*

There's a story of a young philosophy student who goes to see his professor. 'Please help me,' he pleads. 'I've got a question that's eating me alive. I can't sleep through worrying about it. Tell me, do I exist?' The professor turns to him with a withering look and replies, 'Who wants to know?'

With a little reflection, it soon becomes apparent that you are more than just a collection of bones held together by muscle and soft tissue, and more than a collection of thoughts and emotions. Something in you is aware not only of *what* you are thinking but also *that* you are thinking. This is it – the ***Spiritual Self***.

When we realise that we are spiritual beings in human form, it's like waking from a dream. We can step back, see everything in its true perspective, deal with frustration, and find peace and understanding in an imperfect world.

You are now ready for the final breakthrough from which genuine confidence, self-esteem and peace of mind flow.

You are greater than you know, and all is well.

Kahlil Gibran

We can cope with anything if we have the tools and can draw on our inner power. But there is no sun without rain; no joy without spiritual awareness; and no growth without the knowledge that help is always available and we can deal with life's difficulties.

Joy Ward

358 Allow 15-20 minutes for this exercise. Sit or lie down and relax. Notice any physical sensations, then become aware of the one who is observing those sensations. Say, 'I am not these sensations. I am not this body.'

Now be aware of your thinking. Observe your thoughts. Turn your attention to the one who is observing the thoughts. Say, 'I am not these thoughts. I am not my thoughts.'

Then become aware of your emotions. Turn your attention to the one who is observing those emotions. Say, 'I am not these emotions. I am not my emotions.'

Finally become aware of yourself as a spiritual being. Imagine yourself connected to an all powerful Universal Mind that wants the best for you, is guiding and supporting you and bringing you peace. Enjoy this feeling for a few minutes, then open your eyes.

Sit quietly for a few moments before returning to your activities.

359
You can choose peace anytime you wish. Just take a few deep breaths and let them out slowly. Remind yourself that you are a spiritual being, and repeat the affirmation:

'I can choose peace instead of this.'

You cannot be forced to give up your peace of mind unless you are willing to surrender it.

360
At the root of most anxiety is the wish that the world were different. Let go of this and you immediately feel more at peace. *Stop judging.* Display these words on your Wall of Confidence. Make them your prime motto:

Everything is exactly as it should be, and always works out for the best. I am at peace with myself and the world. Nothing and no one can destroy my peace.

361
Give up being dishonest. Confident people have no need to be untruthful, so always keep your word.

For the next 24 hours don't allow a single untruth to pass your lips. Then carry on for another 24 hours and so on. If you fail, just start again and never give up.

362
Live in the present moment and you are well on the way to lasting peace of mind.

Right now, probably all is well in your world, but the moment you allow your thoughts to wander to the past your inner peace is shattered until you bring it back to the present moment.

The only moment over which you have any control is now. Every moment, even the most ordinary is a precious gift. When you're clear on what's really important and focus on what you can do right now, the future has a habit of taking care of itself.

363 Imagine what it would be like if you were connected to a Universal Intelligence that works tirelessly for your benefit, offering you all the confidence you need. Imagine it guiding and supporting you, nourishing your mind and body and taking care of you.

Imagine you could live securely in the knowledge that everything that happens is for your ultimate benefit.

364 Now live as if this were true. Look for your happiness and security in a higher way of thinking. You'll find fear and anxiety fading into oblivion. Life takes on an entire new meaning and you never lack confidence again!

365 This final confidence builder is the secret of a long, happy, confident and fulfilling life.

It comes from the New Testament:

'In love, I live and move and have my being.'

Acts 17:26

I am at one with the Intelligence that created me. I am at peace

If you've worked conscientiously through this book you have taken great strides forward in the last 12 months. You are more self-aware. You know how to set goals, think more confidently, imagine yourself as confident and behave more confidently. If you don't believe me, repeat the marks out of ten exercises (Confidence Builders 8, 9 and 10) and compare these marks with what you gave yourself before.

Occasionally you may have felt yourself slipping back a little from time to time. This is perfectly normal; I call this the 'ratchet effect' – two big steps forward, then one small step back. But if you hang on to your resolve, the overall trend is always upwards. Be patient, keep your eye on the ball, treat setbacks with equanimity and persevere.

I recently spent a fortnight at a holistic holiday centre in Greece where I met a determined young woman who was well on the road to greater confidence and self-esteem. As she reflected on her recent experiences, she uttered the words you will find below. When you become more confident and look back on your life, her sentiments will be yours too.

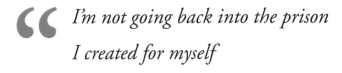 *I'm not going back into the prison I created for myself*

Bibliography

Alan Cohen, *I Had it All the Time*, (Cassette tape programme) Hay House, 1996.

Dr Wayne Dyer, *Your Erroneous Zones*, Warner Books, 1992.

Dr Wayne Dyer, *Pulling Your Own Strings*, Arrow Books, 1978.

Mike George, *The Secrets of Self-Management*, (Cassette tape programme) Brahma Kumaris Information Services Ltd., 2000.

Marcia Grad, *Charisma*, Wilshire Books, 1986.

Dr Susan Jeffers, *Feel The Fear And Do It Anyway*, Arrow Books, 1991.

Gael Lindenfield, *Super Confidence*, Thorsons, 1992.

David Lawrence Preston, *Imagine*, DLP Publications, 2004.

James Redfield, *The Celestine Prophecy*, Bantam Books, 1994.

Martin Shepard, *DIY Psychotherapy*, Vermillion, 1996.

David Swindley, *Only The Truth Shall Set You Free*, Inner Power Publications, 1998.

Ros Taylor et al, *Confidence In Just Seven Days*, Vermilion, 2000.

Eckhart Tolle, *The Power Of Now*, New World Library, 1999.

About the Author

David Lawrence Preston spent 20 years in business and higher education before devoting himself full time to teaching and writing on personal development, and establishing a private psychotherapy and life coaching practice. He is also a staff Development Trainer for Bournemouth Adult Education on the English south coast, and runs courses and seminars on all aspects of confidence and personal and spiritual development. He has appeared many times on radio and television.

David is in the process of producing a set of learning materials to accompany this book.

For further details write (enclosing a stamped addressed envelope or international reply paid coupon) to:

The DLP Hypnotherapy Centre
14 Stanfield Road
Winton
Bournemouth
BH9 2NW.

or visit the DLP web site (http://www.davidlawrencepreston.co.uk) for details of free extracts from David's work.